Taste of Home
5 INGREDIENT *Recipes*

TASTE OF HOME BOOKS • RDA ENTHUSIAST BRANDS, LLC • MILWAUKEE, WI

©2023 RDA Enthusiast Brands, LLC.
1610 N. 2nd St., Suite 102, Milwaukee WI 53212-3906
All rights reserved. Taste of Home is a registered
trademark of RDA Enthusiast Brands, LLC.

Visit us at **tasteofhome.com** for other
Taste of Home books and products.

International Standard Book Number:
978-1-62145-945-3

Component Number:
116700119H

Chief Content Officer, Home & Garden:
Jeanne Sidner
Content Director: Mark Hagen
Creative Director: Raeann Thompson
Senior Editor: Christine Rukavena
Assistant Editor: Sammi DiVito
Senior Designer: Jazmin Delgado
Designer: Carrie Peterson
Deputy Editor, Copy Desk: Dulcie Shoener
Copy Editor: Kara Dennison
Contributing Designer: Jennifer Ruetz

COVER
Photographer: Mark Derse
Set Stylist: Melissa Franco
Food Stylist: Josh Rink

Pictured on front cover:
Skillet Mac & Cheese, p. 44

Pictured on title page:
Beef Steaks with Blue Cheese, p. 63

Pictured on back cover:
Special Pork Chops, p. 65; Sticky Honey Chicken
Wings, p. 22; Berry Dream Cake, p. 99

INSTANT POT is a trademark of Double Insight Inc.
This publication has not been authorized, sponsored
or otherwise approved by Double Insight Inc.

Printed in China
1 3 5 7 9 10 8 6 4 2

BIG KAHUNA
PIZZA, P. 64

NO LONG SHOPPING LISTS—AND NO LONG SHOPPING TRIPS!

For today's busy home cooks, saving time is nearly as important as saving money, and can sometimes seem even harder to do. Luckily, it doesn't take a lot of time or a whole shopping cart full of expensive items to create irresistible homemade meals. Every recipe in this book requires no more than five ingredients and comes together with no fuss, no hassle and no wasted effort.

Whether you're serving up dinner on a busy weeknight, setting out a tasty breakfast to start the day off right, or even planning a party with friends and family, you'll find everything that you're looking for in this savvy yet satisfying collection. Submitted by home cooks from across North America, the recipes in this book will help you create delicious meals your family will love, while keeping your shopping under control. What's more, some recipes here take 30 minutes or less to make, so it's easy to budget both your time and your spending. Plus, every recipe has been tested and approved by the *Taste of Home* Test Kitchen, so you know that they'll come out right the first time.

Homemade breakfasts, quick soups and sandwiches, hearty entrees, fuss-free sides and salads, and lots of satisfying sweets—they're all here for the making. Now, all that's left is to dig in and discover your family's new favorites with **5-Ingredient Recipes**!

172 Recipes Plus Helpful Icons
Keep an eye out for those handy freezer and clock-watching icons! They identify all the recipes in this book that can frozen after cooking and enjoyed later, or the recipes that can be made in 30 minutes (or less), from the time you open the fridge to when you put the meal on the table.

❄ Freezer Friendly

🕒 Fix It Fast

TOASTED COCONUT MILK SHAKES, P. 109

CONTENTS

How Do You Count to Five 4

Breakfast 6

Snacks & Appetizers 20

Breads, Salads & Side Dishes 32

Soups & Sandwiches 46

Main Courses 60

Cookies, Bars, Brownies & Candies 80

Cakes, Pies & Other Desserts 96

Index 111

MORE WAYS TO CONNECT WITH US:

SHOPTASTEOFHOME.COM

GETTING STARTED

HOW DO YOU COUNT TO 5?

You'll notice throughout this book that some recipe lists run longer than five lines. That's because there are a few items that we don't include in our five-ingredient counts. These are essentials that are so basic we feel comfortable assuming every kitchen always has them on hand.

oil

Three oils make our "don't count" list: Vegetable oil, canola oil and regular olive oil. Vegetable and canola oil have a mild flavor and can be used interchangeably. They have a high smoke point, which makes them ideal for frying, sauteing and baking. Regular olive can be used for light sauteing and roasting and for making dressings and sauces. Extra virgin olive oil has more specialized uses due to its low smoke point and will be specified (and counted!) when it's needed for the recipe.

pepper

Black pepper is a go-to kitchen staple, and we don't count it. However, if a recipe calls for freshly cracked black pepper, we will name it and count it. Cracked pepper gives the freshest flavor, but not everyone owns a pepper mill.

salt

When we say "salt," we're referring to traditional table salt, and we don't count it. Many cooks regularly use kosher salt instead, preferring it for its more predictable "pinch" measure—feel free to do so. But if a particular recipe requires kosher salt, we'll name it specifically and include it in our count.

optional ingredients

We also don't include optional items when counting ingredients. We view these items as suggestions—either as garnishes or as a complement—but they aren't necessary to make the recipe, so you can easily leave them out. Also, you can always swap in your own preferred finishing touches if desired.

water

5 Tips for Making the Most of 5 Ingredients

1. Think Fresh

Many of the most famous classic dishes have short ingredient lists and rely on a few distinctive flavors to carry the day. Start with good-quality ingredients and don't overcook, and you won't need a lot of extras.

2. Consider Commercially Available Ingredients That Pile on the Flavor.

You can get a head start on cooking by relying on convenience items such as jarred sauces, packaged rice mixes, seasoning blends, tomatoes with herbs and canned soups.

3. Make Convenience Products Your Own.

Rice, stuffing and pasta mixes are ideal for experimentation. Try adding chopped fresh apple, celery and onion to a stuffing mix, for example, or add shrimp to a rice mix. Take a second look at convenience breads, such as crescent rolls, biscuits and frozen bread dough. You don't have to just make bread with them—they also work with some well-chosen ingredients to make appetizers, casseroles or calzones.

4. Check Out Prepared Foods.

Just because food is already cooked doesn't mean you need to serve it as is! A rotisserie chicken from the deli is the perfect base for your favorite casserole. A package of prepared mashed potatoes gives your shepherd's pie a head start. Or pick up an angel food cake from your store's bakery and turn it into a terrific trifle.

5. Use Mixes in New Ways.

A cake mix can be a good base for cookies or bars. A rice mix can be the starter for a skillet supper. Biscuit and cookie mixes can also provide inspiration for a new recipe.

A WELL-STOCKED KITCHEN

Key to the magic of being able to pull together a great meal on short notice (and prevent an unexpected grocery run) is to have a well-stocked pantry, fridge and freezer. If you cover your bases, you'll always have some things in the kitchen that will work well together. Here are some suggestions for a few basic ingredients to always have on hand.

- All-purpose flour
- Bacon
- Bread or rolls
- Bread crumbs
- Broth or stock (chicken and beef)
- Butter
- Canned beans (garbanzo, cannelini, kidney and/or black)
- Canned tomatoes
- Condensed soups
- Eggs
- Frozen vegetables
- Garlic
- Herbs and spices
- Honey
- Hot sauce/Tabasco sauce
- Lemons
- Milk
- Onions
- Pasta and pasta sauce
- Prepared mustard
- Rice and rice mixes
- Salad dressings
- Salsa
- Shredded cheese (cheddar, Italian blend or Mexican blend)
- Tomato sauce and paste
- Vinegar (red wine, white wine and/or balsamic)

BREAKFAST

**UPSIDE-DOWN BACON
PANCAKE P. 11**

1

2

3

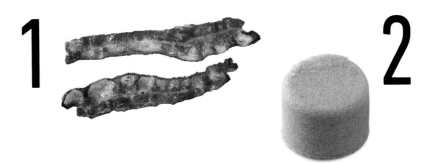

Great Value
Complete
Buttermilk
Pancake &
Waffle Mix

Just add water

NET WT 32 OZ (2 LB) 907g

4

5

Reese.
100% PURE
MAPLE
SYRUP
GRADE A
amber color, rich taste

Net 8 FL OZ (236mL)

DIG INTO DOZENS OF WINNING WAYS TO LOVE THE MOST IMPORTANT MEAL OF THE DAY!

**SPARKLING
PEACH BELLINIS**

ORANGE-GLAZED BACON

You thought bacon couldn't get any tastier, but this recipe is here to surprise you!
—*Taste of Home* Test Kitchen

Prep: 20 min. • **Bake:** 25 min.
Makes: 8 servings

- ¾ cup orange juice
- ¼ cup honey
- 1 Tbsp. Dijon mustard
- ¼ tsp. ground ginger
- ⅛ tsp. pepper
- 1 lb. bacon strips

1. In a small saucepan, combine the first 5 ingredients. Bring to a boil; cook until liquid is reduced to ⅓ cup.
2. Place bacon on a rack in an ungreased 15x10x1-in. baking pan. Bake at 350° for 10 minutes; drain.
3. Drizzle half of glaze over bacon. Bake for 10 minutes. Turn bacon and drizzle with remaining glaze. Bake until golden brown, 5-10 minutes longer. Place bacon on waxed paper until set. Serve warm.
3 glazed bacon strips: 146 cal., 8g fat (3g sat. fat), 21mg chol., 407mg sod., 12g carb. (11g sugars, 0 fiber), 7g pro.

🕐 BANANA CHIP PANCAKES

Perfect for weekends or a special birthday-morning treat, these fluffy pancakes can be customized to your heart's content! One of my kids eats the plain banana pancakes, another likes just chocolate chips added and a third one goes for the works.
—Christeen Kelley, Newark, CA

Takes: 30 min. • **Makes:** 12 pancakes

- 2 cups biscuit/baking mix
- 1 large egg, room temperature
- 1 cup whole milk
- 1 cup mashed ripe bananas
- ¾ cup swirled milk chocolate and peanut butter chips
   Maple syrup and additional swirled milk chocolate and peanut butter chips, optional

1. Place biscuit mix in a large bowl. Whisk the egg, milk and bananas; stir into biscuit mix just until moistened. Stir in chips.
2. Pour batter by ¼ cupfuls onto a greased hot griddle; turn when bubbles form on the top. Cook until the second side of pancake is golden brown. Serve with maple syrup and additional chips if desired.
3 pancakes: 589 cal., 25g fat (16g sat. fat), 59mg chol., 903mg sod., 74g carb. (29g sugars, 3g fiber), 17g pro.

SPARKLING PEACH BELLINIS

Folks will savor the subtle peach flavor in this elegant brunch beverage.
—*Taste of Home* Test Kitchen

Prep: 35 min. + cooling
Makes: 12 servings

- 3 medium peaches, halved
- 1 Tbsp. honey
- 1 can (11.3 oz.) peach nectar, chilled
- 2 bottles (750 ml each) champagne or sparkling grape juice, chilled

1. Line a baking sheet with a large piece of heavy-duty foil (about 18x12 in.). Place peach halves, cut sides up, on foil; drizzle with honey. Fold foil over peach halves and seal.
2. Bake at 375° for 25-30 minutes or until the peaches are tender. Cool completely; remove and discard the peels. In a food processor, process peaches until smooth.
3. Transfer peach puree to a pitcher. Add the nectar and 1 bottle of champagne; stir until combined. Pour into 12 champagne flutes or wine glasses; top with remaining champagne. Serve immediately.
¾ cup: 74 cal., 0 fat (0 sat. fat), 0 chol., 2mg sod., 9g carb. (7g sugars, 1g fiber), 0 pro.

🕐 CUBAN BREAKFAST SANDWICHES

Grab hold of breakfast time by serving these warm, flavorful, energy-boosting Cuban sandwiches. They travel well for busy mornings, and the helping of protein will help keep any hunger at bay.
—Lacie Griffin, Austin, TX

Takes: 20 min. • **Makes:** 4 servings

- 1 loaf (1 lb.) Cuban or French bread
- 4 large eggs
- 16 pieces thinly sliced hard salami
- 8 slices deli ham
- 8 slices Swiss cheese

1. Split bread in half lengthwise; cut into 4 pieces. Fry eggs in a large skillet coated with cooking spray until the yolks are set. Layer the bread bottoms with salami, ham, egg and cheese; replace the tops.
2. Cook on a panini maker or indoor grill for 2 minutes or until bread is browned and cheese is melted.
1 sandwich: 697 cal., 29g fat (12g sat. fat), 280mg chol., 1949mg sod., 61g carb. (1g sugars, 3g fiber), 43g pro.

ORANGE-GLAZED BACON

FRESH CORN OMELET

I throw in homegrown corn and from-scratch salsa when I make this super omelet. Sprinkle on onions, mushrooms, peppers and breakfast meat.
—William Stone, Robson, WV

- -

Takes: 25 min. • **Makes:** 4 servings

- 10 large eggs
- 2 Tbsp. water
- ¼ tsp. salt
- ¼ tsp. pepper
- 2 tsp. plus 2 Tbsp. butter, divided
- 1 cup fresh or frozen corn, thawed
- ½ cup shredded cheddar cheese
  Fresh salsa

1. In a small bowl, whisk eggs, water, salt and pepper until blended. In a nonstick skillet, heat 2 tsp. butter over medium heat. Add corn; cook and stir 1-2 minutes or until tender. Remove from pan.
2. In same pan, heat 1 Tbsp. butter over medium-high heat. Pour in half of the egg mixture. Mixture should set immediately at edges. As eggs set, push cooked portions toward the center, letting uncooked eggs flow underneath. When eggs are thickened and no liquid egg remains, spoon half of the corn on 1 side; sprinkle with ¼ cup cheese. Fold omelet in half. Cut in half; slide each half onto a plate.
3. Repeat with remaining butter, egg mixture and filling. Serve with salsa.
½ omelet: 336 cal., 25g fat (12g sat. fat), 500mg chol., 482mg sod., 8g carb. (3g sugars, 1g fiber), 20g pro.

CHEESY HASH BROWN BAKE

Prepare this cheesy dish ahead of time for less stress on brunch day. You'll love it!
—Karen Burns, Chandler, TX

- -

Prep: 10 min. • **Bake:** 40 min
Makes: 10 servings

- 1 pkg. (30 oz.) frozen shredded hash brown potatoes, thawed
- 2 cans (10¾ oz. each) condensed cream of potato soup, undiluted
- 2 cups sour cream
- 2 cups shredded cheddar cheese, divided
- 1 cup grated Parmesan cheese

1. Preheat oven to 350°. In a large bowl, combine the potatoes, soup, sour cream, 1¾ cups cheddar cheese and Parmesan cheese. Transfer to a greased 3-qt. baking dish. Sprinkle the bake with remaining cheddar cheese.
2. Bake, uncovered, until bubbly and cheese is melted, 40-45 minutes. Let stand 5 minutes before serving.
½ cup: 305 cal., 18g fat (12g sat. fat), 65mg chol., 554mg sod., 21g carb. (3g sugars, 1g fiber), 12g pro.

FRESH CORN
OMELET

GRITS & BACON CASSEROLE

A Mississippi home cook gave me her recipe for grits casserole. It baked like traditional custard. I garnish it with parsley, crumbled bacon and cheese.
—Theresa Liguori, Elkridge, MD

- -

Prep: 20 min. + cooling • **Cook:** 1¼ hours
Makes: 8 servings

- 4½ cups water
- ½ tsp. salt
- ¼ tsp. pepper
- 1 cup quick-cooking grits
- 8 large eggs
- 8 bacon strips, cooked and crumbled
- 1 cup shredded Gouda cheese

1. Preheat oven to 350°. In a saucepan, bring water, salt and pepper to a boil. Slowly stir in the grits. Reduce heat to medium-low; cook, covered, about 5 minutes or until thickened, stirring occasionally. Remove from heat. Pour grits into a greased 2½-qt. souffle dish; cool completely.
2. In a large bowl, whisk eggs; pour over grits. Sprinkle with bacon and cheese.
3. Place casserole in a larger baking pan; add 1 in. of hot water to larger pan. Bake, covered, for 45 minutes. Uncover; bake 30-40 minutes longer or until a knife inserted in the center comes out clean. Let stand 5-10 minutes before serving.
Make-Ahead: Refrigerate the unbaked casserole, covered, for several hours or overnight. To use, preheat the oven to 350°. Remove casserole from refrigerator while the oven heats. Place casserole in a larger baking pan; add 1 in. of hot water to larger pan. Bake, as directed, increasing time as necessary for a knife inserted in the center to come out clean. Let stand 5-10 minutes before serving.
1 piece: 227 cal., 12g fat (5g sat. fat), 210mg chol., 480mg sod., 16g carb. (1g sugars, 1g fiber), 14g pro.

WHISK IT UP
When whisking eggs, tilt the bowl at a 90° angle and whisk from side to side, not in circles.

UPSIDE-DOWN BACON PANCAKE

UPSIDE-DOWN BACON PANCAKE

Make a big impression when you present one family-size bacon pancake. The brown sugar adds sweetness that complements the salty bacon. If you can fit more bacon in the skillet and want to add more, go for it.
—Mindie Hilton, Susanville, CA

- -

Prep: 10 min. • **Bake:** 20 min. + cooling
Makes: 6 servings

- 6 bacon strips, coarsely chopped
- ¼ cup packed brown sugar
- 2 cups complete buttermilk pancake mix
- 1½ cups water
  Optional: Maple syrup and butter

1. In a large cast-iron or other ovenproof skillet, cook bacon over medium heat until crisp. Remove bacon to paper towels with a slotted spoon. Remove the drippings, reserving 2 Tbsp. Return bacon to pan with reserved drippings; sprinkle with brown sugar.
2. In a small bowl, combine the pancake mix and water just until moistened. Pour into pan.
3. Bake at 350° until a toothpick inserted in the center comes out clean, 18-20 minutes. Cool for 10 minutes before inverting onto a serving plate. Serve pancake warm, with maple syrup and butter if desired.
1 slice: 265 cal., 9g fat (3g sat. fat), 12mg chol., 802mg sod., 41g carb. (13g sugars, 1g fiber), 6g pro.

BACON &
EGG GRAVY

⏱ TROPICAL BERRY SMOOTHIES

This fruity, healthy smoothie is a big hit with kids and adults alike because it tastes like a treat while delivering the vitamins. The recipe is easy to increase based on the number of people you'll be serving.
—Hillary Engler, Cape Girardeau, MO

- -

Takes: 10 min. • **Makes:** 2 servings

- 1 cup pina colada juice blend
- 1 container (6 oz.) vanilla yogurt
- ⅓ cup frozen unsweetened strawberries
- ¼ cup frozen mango chunks
- ¼ cup frozen unsweetened blueberries

In a blender, combine all ingredients; cover and process for 30 seconds or until smooth. Pour into chilled glasses; serve immediately.
1¼ cups: 172 cal., 2g fat (1g sat. fat), 4mg chol., 62mg sod., 35g carb. (32g sugars, 2g fiber), 5g pro.

⏱ ZIPPY PRALINE BACON

I'm always looking for recipes to enhance the usual eggs and bacon. My husband came home from a men's brunch raving about this one, and the hostess shared the recipe. Just be sure to make more than you think you might need, because everybody will definitely want seconds!
—Myrt Pfannkuche, Pell City, AL

- -

Takes: 20 min. • **Makes:** 20 pieces

- 1 lb. bacon strips
- 3 Tbsp. brown sugar
- 1½ tsp. chili powder
- ¼ cup finely chopped pecans

1. Preheat oven to 425°. Arrange bacon in a single layer in 2 foil-lined 15x10x1-in. pans. Bake for 10 minutes; carefully pour off drippings.
2. Mix the brown sugar and chili powder; sprinkle over bacon. Sprinkle with pecans. Bake until the bacon is crisp, 5-10 minutes. Drain on paper towels.
1 piece: 58 cal., 4g fat (1g sat. fat), 8mg chol., 151mg sod., 2g carb. (2g sugars, 0 fiber), 3g pro.

⏱ BACON & EGG GRAVY

My husband, Ron, created this breakfast gravy. It's home-style and old-fashioned. Sometimes we like to ladle the gravy over homemade biscuits.
—Terry Bray, Winter Haven, FL

- -

Takes: 20 min. • **Makes:** 2 servings

- 6 bacon strips, diced
- 5 Tbsp. all-purpose flour
- 1½ cups water
- 1 can (12 oz.) evaporated milk
- 3 hard-boiled large eggs, sliced
  Salt and pepper to taste
- 4 slices bread, toasted

In a skillet, cook bacon over medium heat until crisp; remove to paper towels. Stir flour into the drippings until blended; cook over medium heat until browned, stirring constantly. Gradually add water and milk. Bring to a boil; cook and stir for 2 minutes or until thickened. Add bacon, eggs, salt and pepper. Serve over toast.
1 serving: 934 cal., 61g fat (26g sat. fat), 424mg chol., 1030mg sod., 58g carb. (21g sugars, 2g fiber), 33g pro.

⏱ CLASSIC AVOCADO TOAST

This is such an easy way to add avocados to your diet. Use healthy multigrain bread and top with sliced radishes and cracked pepper or lime zest, or chipotle peppers and cilantro.
—Taste of Home Test Kitchen

- -

Takes: 5 min. • **Makes:** 1 serving

- 1 slice hearty bread, toasted
- 1 to 2 tsp. extra virgin olive oil or coconut oil
- ¼ medium ripe avocado, sliced
- ⅛ tsp. sea salt

Spread the toast with olive oil; top with avocado slices. If desired, mash avocado slightly and drizzle with additional oil. Sprinkle with salt.
1 piece: 160 cal., 11g fat (2g sat. fat), 0 chol., 361mg sod., 15g carb. (1g sugars, 3g fiber), 3g pro. **Diabetic exchanges:** 2 fat, 1 starch.

TROPICAL
BERRY SMOOTHIES

**SAUSAGE
BACON BITES**

OVERNIGHT PEACH OATMEAL

Hearty oatmeal combined with sweet peaches make this slow-cooker recipe a perfect breakfast or brunch. This is an excellent meal for busy mornings.
—Rachel Lewis, Danville, VA

Prep: 10 min. • **Cook:** 7 hours
Makes: 6 servings

- 4   cups water
- 1   cup steel-cut oats
- 1   cup vanilla soy milk or vanilla almond milk
- 3   Tbsp. brown sugar
- ¼   tsp. salt
- ¼   tsp. vanilla or almond extract
- 2   medium peaches, sliced or 3 cups frozen unsweetened sliced peaches, thawed
  Optional toppings: Sliced almonds, brown sugar, cinnamon and additional peaches

In a well-greased 3-qt. slow cooker, combine the first 6 ingredients. Cook, covered, on low until oats are tender, 7-8 hours. Stir in sliced peaches just before serving.
Note: Steel-cut oats are also known as Scotch oats or Irish oatmeal.
¾ cup: 163 cal., 2g fat (0 sat. fat), 0 chol., 116mg sod., 31g carb. (13g sugars, 4g fiber), 5g pro. **Diabetic exchanges:** 1½ starch, ½ fruit.
Pressure Cooker Option: Decrease water to 3 cups. Add to a 6-qt. electric pressure cooker coated with cooking spray. Stir in the oats, soy milk, brown sugar, salt and vanilla. Lock lid; close pressure-release valve. Adjust to pressure-cook on high for 4 minutes. Let pressure release naturally. Stir in the peaches just before serving. The oatmeal will thicken upon standing. If desired, top with optional toppings.

HEALTH TIP
Steel-cut oats are 100% whole grain. They are slowly absorbed, giving you energy that will last.

SAUSAGE BACON BITES

These morsels are perfect with almost any egg dish or as finger foods that party guests can just pop in to their mouths.
—Pat Waymire, Yellow Springs, OH

Prep: 20 min. + chilling • **Bake:** 35 min.
Makes: about 3½ dozen

- ¾   lb. sliced bacon
- 2   pkg. (8 oz. each) frozen fully cooked breakfast sausage links, thawed
- ½   cup plus 2 Tbsp. packed brown sugar, divided

1. Preheat oven to 350°. Cut bacon strips widthwise in half; cut sausage links in half. Wrap a piece of bacon around each piece of sausage. Place ½ cup brown sugar in a shallow bowl; roll sausages in sugar. Secure each with a toothpick. Place in a foil-lined 15x10x1-in. baking pan. Cover and refrigerate 4 hours or overnight.
2. Sprinkle with 1 Tbsp. brown sugar. Bake until bacon is crisp, 35-40 minutes, turning once. Sprinkle with remaining brown sugar.
1 piece: 51 cal., 4g fat (1g sat. fat), 6mg chol., 100mg sod., 4g carb. (4g sugars, 0 fiber), 2g pro.

CHEDDAR-HAM OVEN OMELET

We had a family reunion for 50 relatives from the U.S. and Canada, and it took four pans of this hearty, five-ingredient omelet to feed the crowd. Fresh fruit and muffins helped round out our brunch menu.
—Betty Abrey, Imperial, SK

Prep: 15 min. • **Bake:** 40 min. + standing
Makes: 12 servings

- 16   large eggs
- 2   cups whole milk
- 2   cups shredded cheddar cheese
- ¾   cup cubed fully cooked ham
- 6   green onions, chopped

1. Preheat oven to 350°. In a large bowl, whisk eggs and milk. Stir in cheese, ham and onions. Pour into a greased 13x9-in. baking dish.
2. Bake, uncovered, until a knife inserted in center comes out clean, 40-45 minutes. Let stand 10 minutes before cutting.
1 piece: 208 cal., 14g fat (7g sat. fat), 314mg chol., 330mg sod., 4g carb. (3g sugars, 0 fiber), 15g pro.

⏱ CINNAMON TEA ROLLS

Our Test Kitchen used refrigerated crescent rolls to whip up these quick, scrumptious cinnamon treats glazed with a hint of orange.
—*Taste of Home* Test Kitchen

- -

Takes: 20 min. • **Makes:** 4 rolls

- 1   tube (4 oz.) refrigerated crescent rolls
- 1   Tbsp. sugar
- ⅛ tsp. ground cinnamon
- ¼ cup confectioners' sugar
- 1¼ tsp. orange juice

1. Unroll crescent dough into 1 rectangle; seal perforations. Combine sugar and cinnamon; sprinkle over the dough. Roll up jelly-roll style, starting with a short side; pinch seam to seal. Using a serrated knife, cut into 4 slices.
2. Place the rolls, pinched side down, in ungreased muffin cups. Bake at 375° for 10-12 minutes or until golden brown. Cool for 5 minutes before removing from pan to a wire rack. In a small bowl, combine confectioners' sugar and orange juice; drizzle over rolls.
1 serving: 154 cal., 6g fat (2g sat. fat), 0 chol., 223mg sod., 22g carb. (12g sugars, 0 fiber), 2g pro.

⏱ CHERRY SYRUP

My mom and grandma have been making this fruity syrup to serve with fluffy waffles and pancakes ever since I was a little girl. Now I make it for my sons, who love it as much as I do!
—Sandra Harrington, Nipomo, CA

- -

Takes: 30 min. • **Makes:** 3 cups

- 1   pkg. (12 oz.) frozen pitted dark sweet cherries, thawed
- 1   cup water
- 2½ cups sugar
- 2   Tbsp. butter
- ½ tsp. almond extract
     Dash ground cinnamon

1. Bring cherries and water to a boil in a small saucepan. Reduce heat; simmer, uncovered, for 20 minutes.
2. Add sugar and butter; cook and stir until sugar is dissolved. Remove from heat; stir in extract and cinnamon.
3. Cool the leftovers; transfer to airtight containers. Store in the refrigerator for up to 2 weeks.
2 Tbsp.: 100 cal., 1g fat (1g sat. fat), 3mg chol., 7mg sod., 23g carb. (23g sugars, 0 fiber), 0 pro.

CHEESEBURGER
OMELET SLIDER

CHEESEBURGER OMELET SLIDERS

A cheeseburger inside an omelet? Yes, please! This fun twist on two breakfast and dinner faves is easy to assemble and delicious any time of day.
—Denise LaRoche, Hudson, NH

- -

Prep: 25 min. • **Cook:** 25 min.
Makes: 6 servings

- 1   lb. lean ground beef (90% lean)
- 1   tsp. salt, divided
- ½ tsp. pepper, divided
- 8   large eggs
- ½ cup water
- 1   cup shredded Havarti cheese
- 12 dinner rolls, split
- 12 tomato slices
     Optional: Ketchup, sliced onion and pickle slices

1. Combine beef, ½ tsp. salt and ¼ tsp. pepper; mix lightly but thoroughly. Shape into twelve 2-in. patties. In a large skillet, cook burgers over medium heat until cooked through, 2-3 minutes per side. Remove from heat; keep warm.
2. Whisk together the eggs, water and the remaining salt and pepper. Place a small nonstick skillet, lightly oiled, over medium-high heat; pour in ½ cup egg mixture. Mixture should set immediately at edges. As eggs set, push cooked edges toward the center, letting uncooked the eggs flow underneath. When the eggs are thickened and no liquid egg remains, sprinkle ⅓ cup cheese on 1 half. Top the cheese with 3 burgers, spacing them evenly; fold omelet in half. Slide onto a cutting board; tent with foil to keep warm. Repeat to make 3 more omelets.
3. To serve, cut each omelet into 3 wedges; place each wedge on a roll. Add tomatoes and, if desired, ketchup, onion and pickles.
2 sliders: 507 cal., 23g fat (9g sat. fat), 348mg chol., 1032mg sod., 39g carb. (5g sugars, 3g fiber), 34g pro.

CREAMY
BAKED EGGS

⏱ CREAMY BAKED EGGS

My husband loves eggs prepared in any way. This recipe is simple but special, and the eggs come out just as he likes them every time. If you like soft yolks, cook the eggs for 9 minutes; for firmer yolks, cook for about 11 minutes.
—Macey Allen, Green Forest, AR

- -

Takes: 25 min. • **Makes:** 8 servings

- ¼ cup half-and-half cream
- 8 large eggs
- 1 cup shredded Jarlsberg cheese
- 2 Tbsp. grated Parmesan cheese
- ¼ tsp. salt
- ⅛ tsp. pepper
- 2 green onions, chopped

1. Preheat oven to 400°. Pour cream into a greased cast-iron or other ovenproof skillet . Gently break an egg into a small bowl; slip egg into skillet. Repeat with remaining eggs. Sprinkle with cheeses, salt and pepper.

2. Bake until egg whites are completely set and yolks begin to thicken but are not hard, 10-12 minutes. Top with green onions; serve immediately.

1 baked egg: 135 cal., 9g fat (4g sat. fat), 200mg chol., 237mg sod., 2g carb. (1g sugars, 0 fiber), 11g pro.

COCONUT PECAN ROLLS

You're never too busy for fresh-baked sweet rolls when you have this recipe in your morning rotation.
—Theresa Gingry, Blue Springs, NE

- -

Prep: 20 min. • **Bake:** 25 min.
Makes: 8 rolls

- 1 Tbsp. sugar
- ½ tsp. ground cinnamon
- 1 tube (11 oz.) refrigerated breadsticks
- ⅔ cup coconut pecan frosting
- ⅓ cup chopped pecans

1. In a small bowl, combine the sugar and cinnamon. Remove breadstick dough from tube (do not unroll); cut into 8 slices with a serrated knife. Dip both sides of each slice in cinnamon-sugar.

2. Place in a greased 9-in. round baking pan. Spread with frosting; sprinkle with pecans. Bake at 350° until golden brown, 25-30 minutes. Serve warm.

1 serving: 257 cal., 12g fat (3g sat. fat), 0 chol., 330mg sod., 33g carb. (13g sugars, 2g fiber), 3g pro.

BACON BREAKFAST CASSEROLE

BACON BREAKFAST CASSEROLE

This easy breakfast dish helps me make a comforting family favorite that doesn't take a lot of prep. It's also ideal for big brunch gatherings.
—Paula Lawson, Springfield, OH

- -

Prep: 30 min. • **Cook:** 4 hours + standing
Makes: 12 servings

- 1 lb. bacon strips, chopped
- 1 pkg. (28 oz.) frozen O'Brien potatoes, thawed
- 3 cups shredded Mexican cheese blend
- 12 large eggs
- 1 cup 2% milk
- ½ tsp. salt
- ½ tsp. pepper
  Minced fresh parsley, optional

1. In a large skillet, cook bacon in batches over medium heat until crisp. Remove to paper towels to drain.

2. In a greased 4- or 5-qt. slow cooker, layer a third of each of the following: potatoes, reserved bacon and cheese. Repeat the layers twice. In a large bowl, whisk eggs, milk, salt and pepper; pour over top. Cook, covered, on low until eggs are set, 4-5 hours. Turn off slow cooker. Remove the crock insert to a wire rack; let stand, uncovered, 30 minutes before serving. If desired, sprinkle with parsley.

1 serving: 306 cal., 19g fat (8g sat. fat), 226mg chol., 606mg sod., 13g carb. (2g sugars, 2g fiber), 18g pro.

🕐 ❄ BREAKFAST WRAPS

We like quick and simple morning meals during the week, and these wraps can be prepped ahead of time. With just a minute in the microwave, breakfast is ready to go.
—Betty Kleberger, Florissant, MO

Takes: 15 min. • **Makes:** 4 servings

- 6 large eggs
- 2 Tbsp. 2% milk
- ¼ tsp. pepper
- 1 Tbsp. canola oil
- 1 cup shredded cheddar cheese
- ¾ cup diced fully cooked ham
- 4 flour tortillas (8 in.), warmed

1. In a small bowl, whisk the eggs, milk and pepper. In a large skillet, heat oil. Add egg mixture; cook and stir over medium heat until eggs are completely set. Stir in cheese and ham.

2. Spoon egg mixture down the center of each tortilla; roll up.

Freeze option: Wrap cooled egg wrap in foil and freeze in a freezer container. To use, thaw in refrigerator overnight. Remove the foil; wrap the tortilla in a moist paper towel. Microwave on high until heated through, 30-60 seconds. Serve immediately.

1 serving: 436 cal., 24g fat (10g sat. fat), 364mg chol., 853mg sod., 28g carb. (1g sugars, 0 fiber), 25g pro.

Pizza Breakfast Wraps: Prepare recipe as directed, replacing cheddar cheese and ham with mozzarella cheese and cooked sausage. Serve wraps with warm marinara sauce on the side.

Pulled Pork Breakfast Wraps: Prepare the recipe as directed, replacing cheddar cheese and ham with smoked Gouda cheese and precooked pulled pork. Serve with warm barbecue sauce on the side.

🕐 TURKEY BREAKFAST SAUSAGE

These hearty sausage patties are loaded with flavor but contain a fraction of the sodium and fat found in commercial breakfast links.
—Judy Culbertson, Dansville, NY

Takes: 20 min. • **Makes:** 8 servings

- 1 lb. lean ground turkey
- ¾ tsp. salt
- ½ tsp. rubbed sage
- ½ tsp. pepper
- ¼ tsp. ground ginger

1. Crumble the turkey into a large bowl. Add the salt, sage, pepper and ginger; mix lightly but thoroughly. Shape into eight 2-in. patties.

2. In a greased cast-iron or other heavy skillet, cook patties over medium heat until a thermometer reads 165° and the juices run clear, 4-6 minutes on each side.

1 patty: 85 cal., 5g fat (1g sat. fat), 45mg chol., 275mg sod., 0 carb. (0 sugars, 0 fiber), 10g pro. **Diabetic exchanges:** 1 lean meat, ½ fat.

BREAKFAST WRAPS

**GERMAN
POTATO OMELET**

⏱ GERMAN POTATO OMELET

*This is an old German dish that all of us
kids enjoyed when we were growing up.
With a side toast and jam, this flavorful
omelet will make your family as happy
as it made all of us.*
—Katherine Stallwood, Richland, WA

Takes: 30 min. • Makes: 4 servings

- 2 large potatoes, thinly sliced
- ¼ cup butter, divided
- ½ cup sliced green onions
- 8 large eggs
- ¼ cup 2% milk
   Salt and pepper to taste

1. In a large skillet, cook potatoes in 2 Tbsp.
butter for 15 minutes or until browned and
tender. Sprinkle with onions; set aside and
keep warm.

2. In a large nonstick skillet, melt the
remaining butter over medium-high
heat. Whisk the eggs and milk. Add
egg mixture to skillet (mixture should
set immediately at edges).
3. As eggs set, push cooked edges toward
the center, letting uncooked portion flow
underneath. When the eggs are set, spoon
potato mixture on 1 side; fold the other side
over filling. Invert the omelet onto a plate
to serve. Cut into wedges and season
as desired.
1 piece: 400 cal., 22g fat (11g sat. fat),
404mg chol., 253mg sod., 35g carb.
(3g sugars, 4g fiber), 17g pro.

⏱ CALIFORNIA DREAM SMOOTHIE

*It's sunshine in a smoothie! This one's a true
California treat, sweet and tangy from start
to finish.*
—Sonya Labbe, West Hollywood, CA

Takes: 15 min. • Makes: 5 servings

- 2 cups ice cubes
- 1 can (12 oz.) frozen orange
   juice concentrate, thawed
- 1 cup 2% milk
- 1 cup vanilla yogurt
- ½ cup honey

Pulse all ingredients in a blender
until smooth. Serve immediately.
1 cup: 269 cal., 2g fat (1g sat. fat), 6mg chol.,
61mg sod., 61g carb. (57g sugars, 1g fiber),
6g pro.

TEST KITCHEN TIP
For easy cleanup, spritz
the measuring cup with a little
cooking spray before measuring
sticky ingredients like honey
and molasses.

SNACKS & APPETIZERS

**GARLIC-HERB
MINI QUICHES P. 27**

1

2

3

4

5

WHETHER YOU'RE FEEDING A CROWD
OR CRAVING A PICK-ME-UP SNACK,
YOU'LL FIND THE ANSWER HERE.

CANDIED WALNUTS

STICKY HONEY CHICKEN WINGS

This honey chicken wings recipe was given to me by a special lady who was like a grandmother to me.
—Marisa Raponi, Vaughan, ON

Prep: 15 min. + marinating • **Bake:** 30 min.
Makes: 3 dozen

- ½ cup orange blossom honey
- ⅓ cup white vinegar
- 2 Tbsp. paprika
- 2 tsp. salt
- 1 tsp. pepper
- 4 lbs. chicken wings

1. Combine honey, vinegar, paprika, salt and pepper in a small bowl.
2. Cut through the 2 wing joints with a sharp knife, discarding wing tips. Add the remaining wing pieces and honey mixture to a large bowl; stir to coat. Cover; refrigerate 4 hours or overnight.
3. Preheat oven to 375°. Remove wings; reserve honey mixture. Place wings on greased 15x10x1-in. baking pans. Bake until juices run clear, about 30 minutes, turning halfway through.
4. Meanwhile, place reserved honey mixture in a small saucepan. Bring to a boil; cook 1 minute.
5. Remove wings from oven; preheat broiler. Place wings on a greased rack in a broiler pan; brush with the honey mixture. Broil 4-5 in. from heat until crispy, 3-5 minutes. Serve with the remaining honey mixture.
1 piece: 71 cal., 4g fat (1g sat. fat), 16mg chol., 147mg sod., 4g carb. (4g sugars, 0 fiber), 5g pro.

READER REVIEW
"These were a nice change of flavor. They were sticky, gooey and delicious!"
—QUEENLALISA, TASTEOFHOME.COM

🕐 CANDIED WALNUTS

Turn ordinary walnuts into a taste sensation with this easy recipe that's prepared on the stovetop. With plenty of brown sugar and a hint of pepper, the crunchy candied nuts go so well with a fruit-and-cheese tray. But they can stand on their own, as well, since they're so munchable!
—*Taste of Home* Test Kitchen

Takes: 20 min. • **Makes:** 2 cups

- 2 Tbsp. canola oil
- 2 Tbsp. balsamic vinegar
- ⅛ tsp. pepper
- 2 cups walnut halves
- ½ cup packed brown sugar

1. In a large heavy skillet, combine oil, vinegar and pepper. Cook and stir over medium heat until blended. Add walnuts and cook over medium heat until nuts are toasted, about 4 minutes.
2. Sprinkle with brown sugar. Cook and stir until sugar is melted, 2-4 minutes. Spread on foil to cool. Store in an airtight container.
2 Tbsp.: 124 cal., 10g fat (1g sat. fat), 0 chol., 3mg sod., 9g carb. (7g sugars, 1g fiber), 2g pro.

🕐 SPINACH & TURKEY PINWHEELS

Need an awesome snack for game day? My kids love these four-ingredient turkey pinwheels. Go ahead and make them the day before; they won't get soggy!
—Amy Van Hemert, Ottumwa, IA

Takes: 15 min. • **Makes:** 8 servings

- 1 carton (8 oz.) spreadable garden vegetable cream cheese
- 8 flour tortillas (8 in.)
- 4 cups fresh baby spinach
- 1 lb. sliced deli turkey

Spread the cream cheese over tortillas. Layer with spinach and turkey. Roll up tightly; if not serving immediately, cover and refrigerate. To serve, cut the rolls crosswise into 1-in. slices.
6 pinwheels: 307 cal., 13g fat (6g sat. fat), 52mg chol., 866mg sod., 31g carb. (1g sugars, 2g fiber), 17g pro.

STICKY HONEY
CHICKEN WINGS

APPETIZER SHRIMP KABOBS

Talk about fuss-free! These skewers are simple to assemble, and they grill to perfection in minutes. My guests enjoy them with a spicy seafood sauce.
—Dianna Knight, Clayton, NC

Prep: 10 min. + standing • **Grill:** 5 min.
Makes: 8 servings

- 3 Tbsp. olive oil
- 3 garlic cloves, crushed
- ½ cup dry bread crumbs
- ½ tsp. seafood seasoning
- 32 uncooked medium shrimp (about 1 lb.), peeled and deveined
  Seafood cocktail sauce

1. In a shallow bowl, combine the oil and garlic; let stand for 30 minutes. In another bowl, combine bread crumbs and seafood seasoning. Dip shrimp in oil mixture, then coat with crumb mixture.

2. Thread onto metal or soaked wooden skewers. Grill kabobs, covered, over medium heat for 2-3 minutes or until shrimp turn pink. Serve with seafood cocktail sauce.

1 serving: 133 cal., 6g fat (1g sat. fat), 86mg chol., 142mg sod., 6g carb. (0 sugars, 1g fiber), 12g pro. **Diabetic exchanges:** 1½ lean meat, ½ starch.

⏱ SPECIAL STUFFED STRAWBERRIES

These sweet bites can be made ahead of time, and they look really colorful on a tray. I sometimes sprinkle the piped filling with finely chopped pistachio nuts.
—Marcia Orlando, Boyertown, PA

Takes: 20 min. • **Makes:** 2 dozen

- 24 large fresh strawberries
- ½ cup spreadable strawberry cream cheese
- 3 Tbsp. sour cream
  Graham cracker crumbs

1. Place strawberries on a cutting board and cut off tops; remove bottom tips so they sit flat. Using a small paring knife, hull out the center of each berry.

2. In a small bowl, beat cream cheese and sour cream until smooth. Pipe or spoon filling into each berry. Top with crushed graham crackers. Refrigerate until serving.

1 strawberry: 18 cal., 1g fat (1g sat. fat), 4mg chol., 22mg sod., 1g carb. (1g sugars, 0 fiber), 1g pro.

TEST KITCHEN TIP

To make graham cracker crumbs, place graham crackers in a sealed bag and gently crush with the bottom of a bowl or a meat tenderizer.

APPETIZER SHRIMP KABOBS

GINGER-ORANGE REFRESHER

My two-tone drink will impress party guests, with or without the rum. You can use another citrus fruit in place of the oranges if you like.
—Marybeth Mank, Mesquite, TX

Prep: 15 min. • **Cook:** 15 min. + cooling
Makes: 10 servings

- 3 medium oranges
- 1½ cups turbinado (washed raw) sugar
- 1½ cups water
- 1 cup fresh mint leaves
- 8 slices fresh gingerroot
  Crushed ice
- 5 oz. spiced rum, optional
- 1 bottle (1 liter) club soda, chilled

1. Using a vegetable peeler, remove colored layer of peel from oranges in strips, leaving the white pith. Cut the oranges crosswise in half; squeeze juice from oranges.
2. In a small saucepan, combine sugar, water and orange juice; bring to a boil. Stir in the mint, ginger and orange peel; return to a boil. Reduce heat; simmer, uncovered, 10 minutes. Cool the syrup mixture completely.
3. Strain syrup, discarding solids. To serve, fill 10 highball glasses halfway with ice. Add 2 oz. syrup and, if desired, ½ oz. rum to each glass; top with soda.
1 serving: 134 cal., 0 fat (0 sat. fat), 0 chol., 25mg sod., 34g carb. (32g sugars, 1g fiber), 1g pro.

🕐 ROASTED BUFFALO CAULIFLOWER BITES

Try these savory bites for a kickin' appetizer that's healthy, too!
—Emily Tyra, Lake Ann, MI

Takes: 25 min. • **Makes:** 8 servings

- 1 medium head cauliflower (about 2¼ lbs.), cut into florets
- 1 Tbsp. canola oil
- ½ cup Buffalo wing sauce
  Blue cheese salad dressing

1. Preheat oven to 400°. Toss cauliflower with oil; spread in a 15x10x1-in. pan. Roast until the cauliflower is tender and lightly browned, 20-25 minutes, stirring once.
2. Transfer to a bowl; toss with wing sauce. Serve with dressing.
⅓ cup: 39 cal., 2g fat (0 sat. fat), 0 chol., 474mg sod., 5g carb. (2g sugars, 2g fiber), 2g pro.

PROSCIUTTO-WRAPPED ASPARAGUS WITH RASPBERRY SAUCE

🕐 PROSCIUTTO-WRAPPED ASPARAGUS WITH RASPBERRY SAUCE

Grilling the prosciutto with the asparagus gives this appetizer a salty crunch that's perfect for dipping into a sweet glaze. When a delicious appetizer is this easy to prepare, you owe it to yourself to try it!
—Noelle Myers, Grand Forks, ND

Takes: 30 min. • **Makes:** 16 appetizers

- ⅓ lb. thinly sliced prosciutto or deli ham
- 16 fresh asparagus spears, trimmed
- ½ cup seedless raspberry jam
- 2 Tbsp. balsamic vinegar

1. Cut the prosciutto slices in half. Wrap a prosciutto piece around each asparagus spear; secure ends with toothpicks.
2. Grill asparagus, covered, on an oiled rack over medium heat for 6-8 minutes or until prosciutto is crisp, turning once. Discard toothpicks.
3. In a small microwave-safe bowl, microwave jam and vinegar on high for 15-20 seconds or until jam is melted. Serve with asparagus.
1 asparagus spear with 1½ tsp. sauce: 50 cal., 1g fat (0 sat. fat), 8mg chol., 184mg sod., 7g carb. (7g sugars, 0 fiber), 3g pro.
Diabetic exchanges: ½ starch.

SAVORY CUCUMBER SANDWICHES

Italian salad dressing easily flavors this simple snack. You can also omit the bread and serve it as a dip with cucumbers or other veggies.
—Carol Henderson, Chagrin Falls, OH

Prep: 15 min. + chilling • **Makes:** 3 dozen

- 1 pkg. (8 oz.) cream cheese, softened
- ½ cup mayonnaise
- 1 envelope Italian salad dressing mix
- 36 slices snack rye bread
- 1 medium cucumber, sliced
  Snipped fresh dill, optional

1. In a small bowl, combine the cream cheese, mayonnaise and salad dressing mix. Refrigerate for 1 hour.
2. Just before serving, spread over each slice of rye bread; top each with a cucumber slice. If desired, sprinkle with dill.
1 sandwich: 62 cal., 5g fat (2g sat. fat), 7mg chol., 149mg sod., 4g carb. (1g sugars, 0 fiber), 1g pro.

🕐 GARLIC-HERB MINI QUICHES

Looking for a wonderful little bite to dress up the brunch buffet? These delectable tartlets are irresistible!
—Josephine Piro, Easton, PA

Takes: 25 min. • **Makes:** 45 mini quiches

- 1 pkg. (6½ oz.) reduced-fat garlic-herb spreadable cheese
- ¼ cup fat-free milk
- 2 large eggs
- 3 pkg. (1.9 oz. each) frozen miniature phyllo tart shells
- 2 Tbsp. minced fresh parsley
  Minced chives, optional

1. In a small bowl, beat the spreadable cheese, milk and eggs. Place tart shells on an ungreased baking sheet; fill each with 2 tsp. mixture. Sprinkle with parsley.
2. Bake at 350° for 10-12 minutes or until the filling is set and shells are lightly browned. Sprinkle with chives if desired. Serve warm.
1 mini quiche: 31 cal., 2g fat (0 sat. fat), 12mg chol., 32mg sod., 2g carb. (0 sugars, 0 fiber), 1g pro.

SIMMERED SMOKED LINKS

SIMMERED SMOKED LINKS

It's almost impossible to resist the sweet and spicy glaze on these sausages. They are effortless to prepare, and they make the perfect party nibbler. Serve them on frilled toothpicks to make them extra fancy.
—Maxine Cenker, Weirton, WV

Prep: 5 min. • **Cook:** 4 hours
Makes: about 6½ dozen

- 2 pkg. (16 oz. each) miniature smoked sausage links
- 1 cup packed brown sugar
- ½ cup ketchup
- ¼ cup prepared horseradish

Place sausages in a 3-qt. slow cooker. Combine the brown sugar, ketchup and horseradish; pour over sausages. Cover and cook on low for 4 hours.
1 sausage: 46 cal., 3g fat (1g sat. fat), 7mg chol., 136mg sod., 3g carb. (3g sugars, 0 fiber), 1g pro.

HONEY HORSERADISH DIP

We love having appetizers on Friday night instead of a meal, and during the summer we enjoy cooler foods. This has just the right amount of zing.
—Ann Marie Eberhart, Gig Harbor, WA

Prep: 10 min. + chilling • **Makes:** 1 cup

- ½ cup fat-free plain Greek yogurt
- ¼ cup stone-ground mustard
- ¼ cup honey
- 2 Tbsp. prepared horseradish
  Cold cooked shrimp and fresh sugar snap peas

Combine yogurt, mustard, honey and horseradish; refrigerate 1 hour. Serve with shrimp and snap peas.
2 Tbsp.: 54 cal., 1g fat (0 sat. fat), 0 chol., 177mg sod., 11g carb. (10g sugars, 0 fiber), 2g pro. **Diabetic exchanges:** 1 starch.

CHEESY CARAMELIZED ONION SKILLET BREAD

BAKED ASPARAGUS DIP

Since I'm from Wisconsin, I thought it was only logical to put together a vegetable and a cheese.
—Sandra Baratka, Phillips, WI

- -

Takes: 30 min. • **Makes:** about 2 cups

- 1   **lb. diced cooked fresh asparagus, drained**
- 1   **cup grated Parmesan cheese**
- 1   **cup mayonnaise**
      Baked pita chips

In a large bowl, combine the asparagus, cheese and mayonnaise. Place in a 6-in. cast-iron skillet or 2-cup ovenproof bowl. Bake at 375° until heated through, about 20 minutes. Serve warm with pita chips.
2 Tbsp.: 120 cal., 11g fat (2g sat. fat), 5mg chol., 162mg sod., 2g carb. (1g sugars, 0 fiber), 2g pro.

CREAMY WASABI SPREAD

Sesame seeds create an attractive coating for this cracker spread. Be sure to watch when you're toasting them; they burn easily. You'll find rice crackers in the ethnic food aisle. You can use any flavor, but the wasabi ones are fantastic.
—Tammie Balon, Boyce, VA

- -

Takes: 10 min. • **Makes:** 8 servings

- 1   **pkg. (8 oz.) cream cheese**
- ¼   **cup prepared wasabi**
- 2   **Tbsp. sesame seeds, toasted**
- 2   **Tbsp. soy sauce**
      Rice crackers

1. Place cream cheese on a cutting board; split into 2 layers. Spread wasabi over bottom half; replace top layer.
2. Press both sides of cream cheese block into sesame seeds. Place on a shallow serving plate; pour soy sauce around cheese. Serve with rice crackers.
Note: This Japanese version of horseradish is bright green in color and has a pungent, sharp and fiery-hot flavor. It is traditionally used as a condiment served alongside sushi and sashimi. Today, many Western sauces, mustards and other condiments are seasoned with wasabi. Wasabi powder and paste are also available in the Asian food section of the grocery store.
1 oz.: 135 cal., 11g fat (6g sat. fat), 31mg chol., 483mg sod., 6g carb. (0 sugars, 0 fiber), 3g pro.

CHEESY CARAMELIZED ONION SKILLET BREAD

This appetizer is perfect for a football game or informal party, but it came about because I have two sons who are always so hungry. They love the skillet bread for the flavor, and I love it because it keeps them in the kitchen to chat while I prepare the rest of dinner! If you'd like, you can use homemade biscuits instead of prepared.
—Mary Leverette, Columbia, SC

- -

Prep: 45 min. • **Bake:** 20 min.
Makes: 8 servings

- 2   **tsp. caraway seeds**
- 1   **Tbsp. olive oil**
- 1   **large onion, chopped**
- ¼   **tsp. salt**
- 1   **cup shredded sharp cheddar cheese**
- ½   **cup butter, melted**
- 1   **tube (16.3 oz.) large refrigerated buttermilk biscuits**
- 1   **Tbsp. minced fresh thyme, optional**

1. Preheat oven to 350°. In a 10-in. cast-iron or other ovenproof skillet, toast the caraway seeds until fragrant, for about 1 minute.
2. Remove and set aside. In the same skillet, heat oil over medium heat. Add the onion; cook and stir until softened, 5-6 minutes. Reduce heat to medium-low and cook until deep golden brown, 30-40 minutes, stirring occasionally. Stir in salt; remove from the heat and cool slightly.
3. Sprinkle cheese over onions in skillet. Place melted butter and caraway seeds in a shallow bowl. Cut each biscuit into fourths. Dip the biscuit pieces in butter mixture; place in a single layer over the onion mixture in skillet.
4. Bake until puffed and golden brown, 20-25 minutes. Cool in skillet 5 minutes before inverting onto a serving plate. If desired, sprinkle with fresh thyme. Serve warm.
1 serving: 352 cal., 25g fat (13g sat. fat), 45mg chol., 874mg sod., 27g carb. (4g sugars, 1g fiber), 7g pro.

SPARKLING COCONUT
GRAPE JUICE

SLOW-COOKER CHEESE DIP

I brought this slightly spicy cheese dip to a gathering with friends and it was a huge hit. The spicy pork sausage provides the zip!
—Marion Bartone, Conneaut, OH

- -

Prep: 15 min. • **Cook:** 4 hours
Makes: 32 servings (2 qt.)

- 1 lb. ground beef
- ½ lb. bulk spicy pork sausage
- 2 lbs. cubed Velveeta
- 2 cans (10 oz. each) diced tomatoes and green chiles
  Tortilla chip scoops, red pepper and cucumber sticks

1. In a large skillet, cook beef and sausage over medium heat until no longer pink; drain. Transfer to a 3- or 4-qt. slow cooker. Stir in cheese and tomatoes.
2. Cover and cook on low for 4-5 hours or until the cheese is melted, stirring occasionally. Serve with tortilla chips, red pepper and cucumber sticks.
¼ cup: 139 cal., 10g fat (5g sat. fat), 40mg chol., 486mg sod., 3g carb. (2g sugars, 0 fiber), 8g pro

🕐 SPARKLING COCONUT GRAPE JUICE

This sparkling drink is a nice change of pace from lemonade and party punch. The lime, coconut and grape combo is so refreshing. Add a splash of gin if you're feeling bold.
—Shelly Bevington, Hermiston, OR

- -

Takes: 5 min. • **Makes:** 6 servings

- 4 cups white grape juice
- 2 tsp. lime juice
  Ice cubes
- 2 cups coconut-flavored sparkling water, chilled
  Optional: Lime wedges or slices

In a pitcher, combine grape juice and lime juice. Fill 6 tall glasses with ice. Pour juice mixture evenly into glasses; top off with sparkling water. Stir to combine. Garnish with lime wedges if desired.
1 cup: 94 cal., 0 fat (0 sat. fat), 0 chol., 13mg sod., 24g carb. (21g sugars, 0 fiber), 0 pro.

DID YOU KNOW?
You can often use lemon and lime juice (and peel) interchangeably in recipes to achieve a different flavor.

MARINARA-MOZZARELLA DIP

APPLE-GOUDA PIGS IN A BLANKET

For New Year's, I used to make beef and cheddar pigs in a blanket, but now I like to use apple and Gouda for an even better flavor celebration.
—Megan Weiss, Menomonie, WI

Takes: 30 min. • **Makes:** 2 dozen

- 1 tube (8 oz.) refrigerated crescent rolls
- 1 small apple, peeled and cut into 24 thin slices
- 6 thin slices Gouda cheese, quartered
- 24 miniature smoked sausages Honey mustard salad dressing, optional

1. Preheat oven to 375°. Unroll crescent dough and separate into 8 triangles; cut each lengthwise into 3 thin triangles. On the wide end of each triangle, place 1 slice apple, 1 folded piece cheese and 1 sausage; roll up tightly.
2. Place 1 in. apart on parchment-lined baking sheets, point side down. Bake for 10-12 minutes or until golden brown. If desired, serve with dressing.
1 appetizer: 82 cal., 6g fat (2g sat. fat), 11mg chol., 203mg sod., 5g carb. (1g sugars, 0 fiber), 3g pro.

CHILI & JELLY MEATBALLS

The secret ingredient in this sassy sauce is the grape jelly. It's a sweet contrast with the chili sauce.
—Irma Schnuelle, Manitowoc, WI

Takes: 30 min. • **Makes:** about 3 dozen

- 2 pkg. (22 oz. each) frozen fully cooked angus beef meatballs
- 1 bottle (12 oz.) chili sauce
- 1 jar (10 oz.) grape jelly

1. Prepare the meatballs according to package instructions.
2. In a large skillet, combine chili sauce and jelly; cook and stir over medium heat until jelly has melted. Add the meatballs to pan; heat through.
1 meatball: 106 cal., 6g fat (3g sat. fat), 17mg chol., 313mg sod., 8g carb. (6g sugars, 0 fiber), 4g pro.

MARINARA-MOZZARELLA DIP

Talk about easy! With three ingredients and two loaves of baguette-style French bread, you have an easy appetizer that will please your family and guests. For variation, try using goat cheese instead of mozzarella.
—Janie Colle, Hutchinson, KS

Prep: 10 min. • **Cook:** 2½ hours
Makes: 12 servings (3 cups)

- 2 cups marinara sauce
- 1 carton (8 oz.) fresh mozzarella cheese pearls, drained
- 2 Tbsp. minced fresh basil French bread baguette, thinly sliced and toasted Optional: Crushed red pepper flakes and additional fresh minced basil

Pour marinara into a 1½-qt. slow cooker. Cook, covered, on low about 2 hours, until hot. Stir in mozzarella and basil. Cook until cheese is melted, about 30 minutes longer. If desired, top with red pepper flakes and additional basil. Serve with the toasted baguette slices.
¼ cup: 76 cal., 5g fat (3g sat. fat), 16mg chol., 219mg sod., 4g carb. (3g sugars, 1g fiber), 4g pro.

TEST KITCHEN TIP

This recipe works well with jarred pasta sauce, so use your favorite brand and flavor.

APPLE-GOUDA
PIGS IN A BLANKET

BREADS, SALADS & SIDE DISHES

SKILLET MAC & CHEESE
P. 44

1

2

3

4

5

ROUND OUT YOUR MEAL WITH ONE OF THE
DELICIOUS, SAVORY DISHES IN THIS GO-TO CHAPTER.

SIMPLE
BISCUITS

⏱ SIMPLE BISCUITS

It's super easy to whip up a batch of these buttery biscuits to serve with breakfast or dinner. The dough is very easy to work with, so there's no need to roll with a rolling pin; just pat to the right thickness.
—*Taste of Home* Test Kitchen

Takes: 25 min. • **Makes:** 15 biscuits

- 2 cups all-purpose flour
- 3 tsp. baking powder
- 1 tsp. salt
- ⅓ cup cold butter, cubed
- ⅔ cup 2% milk

1. Preheat oven to 450°. In a large bowl, whisk flour, baking powder and salt. Cut in butter until mixture resembles coarse crumbs. Add milk; stir just until moistened.
2. Turn onto a lightly floured surface; knead gently 8-10 times. Pat dough to ½-in. thickness. Cut with a 2½-in. biscuit cutter.
3. Place 1 in. apart on an ungreased baking sheet. Bake until golden brown, 10-15 minutes. Serve warm.
1 biscuit: 153 cal., 7g fat (4g sat. fat), 18mg chol., 437mg sod., 20g carb. (1g sugars, 1g fiber), 3g pro.

CREAMY JALAPENO CORN

My version of creamed corn gets its spicy kick from jalapeno peppers. Try a chopped poblano or small red bell pepper for a more mild side dish.
—Judy Carty, Wichita, KS

Prep: 15 min. • **Cook:** 4 hours
Makes: 8 servings

- 2 pkg. (16 oz. each) frozen corn
- 1 pkg. (8 oz.) cream cheese, softened and cubed
- 4 jalapeno peppers, seeded and finely chopped
- ¼ cup butter, cubed
- 2 Tbsp. water
- ½ tsp. salt
- ¼ tsp. pepper

In a 3-qt. slow cooker, combine all the ingredients. Cover; cook on low until the corn is tender, stirring occasionally, 4-5 hours.
Note: Wear disposable gloves when cutting hot peppers; the oils can burn skin. Avoid touching your face.
¾ cup: 251 cal., 16g fat (10g sat. fat), 46mg chol., 275mg sod., 25g carb. (2g sugars, 3g fiber), 6g pro.

BUTTERY CARROTS

⏱ BUTTERY CARROTS

My mother made this recipe often when I was growing up. She got it from a friend who was a chef at a local restaurant my parents frequented. The onions really bring out the sweetness of the carrots. When I have carrots fresh from the garden, I don't even peel them—I just scrub them well before cutting. For holiday buffets, I often double or triple this recipe.
—Mary Ellen Chambers, Lakewood, OH

Takes: 20 min. • **Makes:** 12 servings

- 3 lbs. medium carrots, halved crosswise and cut into strips
- 2 medium onions, halved and thinly sliced
- ½ cup butter, melted
- ½ cup chopped fresh parsley
- ½ tsp. salt
   Coarsely ground pepper, optional

1. Fill 6-qt. stockpot with 2 in. water. Add the carrots and onions; bring to a boil. Reduce heat; simmer, covered, until the sliced carrots are crisp-tender, 10-12 minutes.
2. Drain vegetables. Toss with remaining ingredients.
¾ cup: 123 cal., 8g fat (5g sat. fat), 20mg chol., 240mg sod., 13g carb. (6g sugars, 4g fiber), 1g pro.

TEST KITCHEN TIP
To keep parsley fresh for up to a month, trim the stems and place the bunch in a tumbler with an inch of water. Be sure no loose leaves are in the water. Tie a produce bag around the tumbler to trap humidity; store in the refrigerator. Each time you use parsley, change the water.

**PRESSURE-COOKER
BUFFALO WING POTATOES**

CREAMY SKILLET NOODLES WITH PEAS

I've made this noodle side for years. Since kids and adults go for it, I keep the ingredients on hand at all times.
—Anita Groff, Perkiomenville, PA

Takes: 25 min. • **Makes:** 6 servings

- ¼ cup butter, cubed
- 2 Tbsp. canola oil
- 5 cups uncooked fine egg noodles
- 2½ cups frozen peas (about 10 oz.)
- 2½ cups chicken broth
- 1 cup half-and-half cream
- ½ tsp. salt
- ¼ tsp. pepper

In a large skillet, heat butter and oil over medium heat. Add noodles; cook and stir 2-3 minutes or until lightly browned. Stir in peas, broth, cream, salt and pepper. Bring to a boil. Reduce heat; simmer, covered, 10-12 minutes or until noodles are tender, stirring occasionally.
¾ cup: 329 cal., 31g fat (8g sat. fat), 76mg chol., 757mg sod., 31g carb. (6g sugars, 4g fiber), 9g pro.

PEAR & BLUE CHEESE SALAD

This crisp fall salad gets its tartness from fresh pears, an extra crunch from pecans and a hint of creaminess from blue cheese. It's simple, but always impresses.
—*Taste of Home* Test Kitchen

Takes: 10 min. • **Makes:** 10 servings

- 12 cups torn romaine
- ⅔ cup balsamic vinaigrette
- 2 medium pears, sliced
- ⅔ cup crumbled blue cheese
- ⅔ cup glazed pecans

Place romaine in a large bowl. Drizzle with vinaigrette; toss to coat. Top with the pears, cheese and pecans. Serve salad immediately.
1 cup: 133 cal., 8g fat (2g sat. fat), 7mg chol., 324mg sod., 12g carb. (8g sugars, 3g fiber), 3g pro. **Diabetic exchanges:** 1½ fat, 1 vegetable, ½ starch.

PRESSURE-COOKER BUFFALO WING POTATOES

I was getting tired of mashed potatoes and baked spuds, so I decided to create something new. This potluck-ready recipe is an easy and delicious twist on the usual potato dish.
—Summer Feaker, Ankeny, IA

Takes: 20 min. • **Makes:** 6 servings

- 2 lbs. Yukon Gold potatoes, cut into 1-in. cubes
- 1 small sweet yellow pepper, chopped
- ½ small red onion, chopped
- ¼ cup Buffalo wing sauce
- ½ cup shredded cheddar cheese
  Optional toppings: Crumbled cooked bacon, sliced green onions and sour cream

1. Place steamer basket and 1 cup water in a 6-qt. electric pressure cooker. Set the potatoes, yellow pepper and onion in basket. Lock lid; close pressure-release valve. Adjust to pressure-cook on high for 3 minutes. Quick-release pressure.
2. Remove vegetables to a serving bowl; discard cooking liquid. Add Buffalo wing sauce to vegetables; gently stir to coat. Sprinkle with the cheese. Cover and let stand until cheese is melted, 1-2 minutes. If desired, top with bacon, green onions and sour cream.
¾ cup: 182 cal., 4g fat (2g sat. fat), 9mg chol., 382mg sod., 32g carb. (3g sugars, 3g fiber), 6g pro. **Diabetic exchanges:** 2 starch, ½ fat.

BROCCOLI WITH GARLIC, BACON & PARMESAN

A few simple ingredients make ordinary broccoli irresistible.
—Erin Chilcoat, Central Islip, NY

- -

Takes: 30 min. • **Makes:** 8 servings

- 1 tsp. salt
- 2 bunches broccoli (about 3 lbs.), stems removed, cut into florets
- 6 thick-sliced bacon strips, chopped
- 2 Tbsp. olive oil
- 6 to 8 garlic cloves, thinly sliced
- ½ tsp. crushed red pepper flakes
- ¼ cup shredded Parmesan cheese

1. Fill a 6-qt. stockpot two-thirds full with water; add salt and bring to a boil over high heat. In batches, add broccoli and cook until the broccoli turns bright green, 2-3 minutes; remove the broccoli with a slotted spoon.
2. In a large skillet, cook bacon strips over medium heat until crisp, stirring occasionally. Remove with a slotted spoon; drain on paper towels. Discard drippings, reserving 1 Tbsp. in pan.
3. Add olive oil to drippings; heat over medium heat. Add garlic and pepper flakes; cook and stir until the garlic is fragrant, 2-3 minutes (do not allow to brown). Add the broccoli; cook until broccoli is tender, stirring occasionally. Stir in bacon; sprinkle with cheese.
¾ cup: 155 cal., 10g fat (3g sat. fat), 11mg chol., 371mg sod., 11g carb. (3g sugars, 4g fiber), 8g pro. **Diabetic exchanges:** 2 fat, 1 vegetable.

MILK-AND-HONEY
WHITE BREAD

MILK-AND-HONEY WHITE BREAD

Honey adds special flavor to this traditional white bread.
—Kathy McCreary, Goddard, KS

- -

Prep: 15 min. + rising • **Bake:** 30 min.
Makes: 2 loaves (16 slices each)

- 2 pkg. (¼ oz. each) active dry yeast
- 2½ cups warm whole milk (110° to 115°)
- ⅓ cup honey
- ¼ cup butter, melted
- 2 tsp. salt
- 8 to 8½ cups all-purpose flour

1. In a large bowl, dissolve yeast in warm milk. Add honey, butter, salt and 5 cups flour; beat until smooth. Add enough remaining flour to form a soft dough.
2. Turn onto a floured board; knead until smooth and elastic, 6-8 minutes. Place in a greased bowl, turning once to grease top. Cover and let rise in a warm place until doubled, about 1 hour.
3. Punch dough down and shape into 2 loaves. Place in greased 9x5-in. loaf pans. Cover and let rise until doubled, about 30 minutes.
4. Bake at 375° for 30-35 minutes or until golden brown. Cover loosely with foil if top browns too quickly. Remove from pans and cool on wire racks.
1 piece: 149 cal., 2g fat (1g sat. fat), 6mg chol., 172mg sod., 28g carb. (4g sugars, 1g fiber), 4g pro.

SLOW-COOKED POTATOES WITH SPRING ONIONS

AMBROSIA SALAD

Because it's so very simple to make, this tropical medley is ideal as a last-minute menu addition. Plus, it requires just five easy ingredients.
—Judi Bringegar, Liberty, NC

Prep: 10 min. + chilling
Makes: 4 servings

- 1 can (15 oz.) mandarin oranges, drained
- 1 can (8 oz.) pineapple tidbits, drained
- 1 cup miniature marshmallows
- 1 cup sweetened shredded coconut
- 1 cup sour cream

In a large bowl, combine the oranges, pineapple, marshmallows and coconut. Add sour cream and toss to mix. Cover and refrigerate for several hours.
1 cup: 370 cal., 20g fat (14g sat. fat), 14mg chol., 101mg sod., 48g carb. (43g sugars, 2g fiber), 4g pro.

🕐 CHEESY BACON SPAGHETTI SQUASH

This quick casserole is called cheesy for a reason. Stir in any kind you've got.
—Jean Williams, Stillwater, OK

Takes: 30 min. • **Makes:** 4 servings

- 1 large spaghetti squash (3½ lbs.)
- 4 bacon strips, chopped
- 3 Tbsp. butter
- 1 Tbsp. brown sugar
- ½ tsp. salt
- ¼ tsp. pepper
- ½ cup shredded Swiss cheese

1. Halve the squash lengthwise; discard seeds. Place squash on a microwave-safe plate, cut side down; microwave on high until tender, 15-20 minutes. Cool slightly. Separate strands with a fork.
2. In a large skillet, cook the bacon strips over medium heat until crisp, stirring occasionally. With a slotted spoon, remove the bacon to paper towels; reserve drippings.
3. In same pan, heat the drippings over medium heat; stir in butter, brown sugar, salt and pepper until blended. Add the squash; toss and heat through. Remove from heat; stir in cheese. Top with bacon.
Note: This recipe was tested in a 1,100-watt microwave.
1 cup: 381 cal., 26g fat (12g sat. fat), 54mg chol., 627mg sod., 32g carb. (4g sugars, 6g fiber), 10g pro.

SLOW-COOKED POTATOES WITH SPRING ONIONS

I love the simplicity of this recipe, as well as the ease of preparation with my slow cooker. Everyone always likes roasted potatoes, even my pickiest child! If desired, top with shredded or crumbled cheese.
—Theresa Gomez, Stuart, FL

Prep: 5 min. • **Cook:** 6 hours
Makes: 12 servings

- 4 lbs. small red potatoes
- 8 green onions, chopped (about 1 cup)
- 1 cup chopped sweet onion
- ¼ cup olive oil
- ½ tsp. salt
- ½ tsp. pepper

In a 5- or 6-qt. slow cooker, combine all ingredients. Cook, covered, on low until potatoes are tender, 6-8 hours.
1 serving: 157 cal., 5g fat (1g sat. fat), 0 chol., 110mg sod., 26g carb. (2g sugars, 3g fiber), 3g pro. **Diabetic exchanges:** 1½ starch, 1 fat.

🕐 PINA COLADA CARROT SALAD

This carrot salad with pina colada yogurt, green grapes and macadamia nuts has a tropical theme. Just mix and chill out.
—Emily Tyra, Lake Ann, MI

Takes: 10 min. • **Makes:** 4 servings

- 1 pkg. (10 oz.) julienned carrots
- 1 cup green grapes, halved
- ¾ cup pina colada yogurt
- ⅓ cup salted dry roasted macadamia nuts, chopped
  Lemon wedges

In a large bowl, combine carrots, grapes, yogurt and macadamia nuts; toss to coat. Squeeze the lemon wedges over salad before serving.
¾ cup: 184 cal., 9g fat (2g sat. fat), 2mg chol., 157mg sod., 24g carb. (19g sugars, 3g fiber), 3g pro. **Diabetic exchanges:** 1½ fat, 1 starch, 1 vegetable.

AMBROSIA
SALAD

⏱ PLANTAIN FRITTERS

These golden brown plantain fritters are a favorite in West Africa, where my aunt served as a missionary for 45 years. Make sure the plantains are very ripe, or use bananas instead.
—Heather Ewald, Bothell, WA

Takes: 20 min. • **Makes:** 2 dozen

- 2 large ripe plantains or bananas, peeled
- 1 cup self-rising flour
- 1 small onion, cut into wedges
- ¼ tsp. salt
  Dash pepper
  Oil for deep-fat frying

1. Place plantains in a food processor; cover and process until smooth. Add the flour, onion, salt and pepper; cover and process until blended (batter will be moist).

2. In an electric skillet or deep-fat fryer, heat ¼ in. of oil to 375°. Drop tablespoonfuls of batter, a few at a time, into hot oil. Cook until golden brown, 1 minute on each side. Drain on paper towels.

Note: As a substitute for 1 cup of self-rising flour, place 1½ tsp. baking powder and ½ tsp. salt in a measuring cup. Add all-purpose flour to measure 1 cup.

1 fritter: 77 cal., 5g fat (0 sat. fat), 0 chol., 87mg sod., 9g carb. (2g sugars, 1g fiber), 1g pro.

⏱ INSALATA CAPRESE

The colors in a classic Caprese salad resemble the Italian flag. For extra zing, I like to add a splash of balsamic vinegar.
—Joe Colamonico, North Charleston, SC

Takes: 25 min. • **Makes:** 8 servings

- 2½ lbs. plum tomatoes (about 10), cut into 1-in. pieces
- 1 carton (8 oz.) fresh mozzarella cheese pearls
- ½ cup pitted ripe olives
- 3 Tbsp. olive oil
- ¼ cup thinly sliced fresh basil
- 2 tsp. minced fresh oregano
- ½ tsp. salt
- ¼ tsp. pepper
  Balsamic vinegar, optional

In a large bowl, mix tomatoes, cheese pearls and olives. Drizzle with the oil. Sprinkle with basil, oregano, salt and pepper; toss to coat. Let salad stand 10 minutes before serving. If desired, drizzle with vinegar.

¾ cup: 160 cal., 12g fat (5g sat. fat), 22mg chol., 257mg sod., 7g carb. (4g sugars, 2g fiber), 6g pro.

READER REVIEW
"Just perfect! I used cherry tomatoes and cut them in half. I did add the balsamic vinegar, and it was so good with the fresh herbs."
—DEBORAHLZ, TASTEOFHOME.COM

PLANTAIN FRITTERS

GARLIC LOAF

This golden loaf has garlicky goodness in every bite. People go wild over its savory flavor. Try serving it with an herb-infused or lightly salted olive oil for dunking.
—*Taste of Home* Test Kitchen

- -

Prep: 15 min. + rising • **Bake:** 20 min.
Makes: 1 loaf (24 pieces)

2 loaves (1 lb. each) frozen bread dough or 24 frozen unbaked white dinner rolls, thawed
½ cup finely chopped sweet onion
½ cup butter, melted
2 garlic cloves, minced
1 tsp. dried parsley flakes
¼ tsp. salt
   Herb-seasoned olive oil, optional

1. Divide dough into 24 pieces. In a small bowl, combine the onion, butter, garlic, parsley and salt. Dip each piece of dough into butter mixture; place in a 10-in. fluted tube pan coated with cooking spray. Cover and let rise in a warm place until doubled, about 1 hour.
2. Bake at 375° for 20-25 minutes or until golden brown. Serve warm, with olive oil if desired.
1 piece: 141 cal., 5g fat (2g sat. fat), 10mg chol., 263mg sod., 19g carb. (2g sugars, 2g fiber), 4g pro.

STRAWBERRY FETA
TOSSED SALAD

OVEN-ROASTED POTATOES

Some rosemary, fresh or dried, gives these potatoes a distinctive and subtle taste. This dish is simple to prepare, yet elegant in color and flavor. It's such a wonderful addition to any menu.
—Margie Wampler, Butler, PA

- -

Takes: 30 min. • **Makes:** 8 servings

2 lbs. small unpeeled red potatoes, cut into wedges
2 to 3 Tbsp. olive oil
2 garlic cloves, minced
1 Tbsp. minced fresh rosemary or 1 tsp. dried rosemary, crushed
½ tsp. salt
¼ tsp. pepper

1. Place potatoes in a 13x9-in. baking dish. Drizzle with oil. Sprinkle with the garlic, rosemary, salt and pepper; toss gently to coat.
2. Bake at 450° until potatoes are golden brown and tender, 20-30 minutes.
1 cup: 114 cal., 4g fat (0 sat. fat), 0 chol., 155mg sod., 18g carb. (1g sugars, 2g fiber), 2g pro.

STRAWBERRY FETA TOSSED SALAD

A neighbor served this wonderful salad at a barbecue. I've since experimented with many ingredient combinations, but this one draws the most compliments. I took it to a baby shower, and not a seed was left in the bowl.
—Lisa Lesinski-Topp, Menomonee Falls, WI

- -

Takes: 10 min. • **Makes:** 6 servings

6 cups torn mixed salad greens
2 cups fresh strawberries, sliced
1 pkg. (4 oz.) crumbled feta cheese
¼ cup sunflower kernels
   Balsamic vinaigrette

Place first 4 ingredients in a large bowl. To serve, drizzle with vinaigrette; toss to combine.
1 cup: 103 cal., 6g fat (2g sat. fat), 10mg chol., 259mg sod., 8g carb. (3g sugars, 3g fiber), 6g pro.

CREAMED CORN

Five ingredients are all you'll need for my popular dinner accompaniment. It's so wonderful no matter what the occasion is. Try it on a barbecue buffet or holiday menu.
—Barbara Brizendine, Harrisonville, MO

- -

Prep: 10 min. • **Cook:** 3 hours
Makes: 5 servings

2 pkg. (one 16 oz., one 10 oz.) frozen corn
1 pkg. (8 oz.) cream cheese, softened and cubed
¼ cup butter, cubed
1 Tbsp. sugar
½ tsp. salt

In a 3-qt. slow cooker coated with cooking spray, combine all ingredients. Cover and cook on low for 3 to 3½ hours or until the cheese is melted and corn is tender. Stir just before serving.
¾ cup: 378 cal., 26g fat (16g sat. fat), 74mg chol., 439mg sod., 34g carb. (5g sugars, 4g fiber), 8g pro.

MINTY PEAS
& ONIONS

⏱ MINTY PEAS & ONIONS

Mother always relied on peas and onions when she was in a hurry and needed a quick side dish. Besides being easy to prepare, this dish was extremely loved by our family. My grandmother handed it down to my mother.
—Santa D'Addario, Jacksonville, FL

Takes: 20 min. • **Makes:** 8 servings

- 2 large onions, cut into ½-in. wedges
- ½ cup chopped sweet red pepper
- 2 Tbsp. vegetable oil
- 2 pkg. (16 oz. each) frozen peas
- 2 Tbsp. minced fresh mint or 2 tsp. dried mint

In a large skillet, saute the onions and red pepper in oil until the onions just begin to soften. Add peas; cook, uncovered, stirring occasionally, for 10 minutes or until heated through. Stir in mint and cook for 1 minute.
1 serving: 134 cal., 4g fat (1g sat. fat), 0 chol., 128mg sod., 19g carb. (9g sugars, 6g fiber), 6g pro. **Diabetic exchanges:** 1 starch, 1 fat.

RANCH POTATO SALAD

I jazzed up creamy potato salad with cheese, bacon and ranch salad dressing. My sister asked for the recipe as soon as she tried it.
—Lynn Breunig, Wind Lake, WI

Prep: 30 min. + chilling
Makes: 8 servings

- 2 lbs. red potatoes
- 1 bottle (8 oz.) ranch salad dressing
- 1 cup shredded cheddar cheese
- 1 pkg. (2.8 oz.) bacon bits
- ¼ tsp. pepper
  Dash garlic powder

1. Place potatoes in a large saucepan and cover with water. Bring to a boil. Reduce heat; cover and simmer until tender, 20-25 minutes.
2. In a large bowl, combine the remaining ingredients (dressing will be thick). Drain the potatoes and cut into cubes; add to dressing and gently toss to coat. Cover and refrigerate for 2 hours or until the salad is chilled. Refrigerate leftovers.
1 cup: 316 cal., 22g fat (6g sat. fat), 27mg chol., 649mg sod., 20g carb. (2g sugars, 2g fiber), 9g pro.

GRANDMOTHER'S
ORANGE SALAD

GRANDMOTHER'S ORANGE SALAD

This slightly sweet gelatin salad is a little bit tangy, too. It adds beautiful color to any meal and appeals to all ages.
—Ann Eastman, Santa Monica, CA

Prep: 20 min. + chilling
Makes: 10 servings

- 1 can (11 oz.) mandarin oranges
- 1 can (8 oz.) crushed pineapple
  Water
- 1 pkg. (6 oz.) orange gelatin
- 1 pint orange sherbet, softened
- 2 bananas, sliced

1. Drain oranges and pineapple, reserving juices. Set oranges and pineapple aside. Add water to juices to measure 2 cups. Place in a saucepan and bring to a boil; pour over gelatin in a large bowl. Stir until gelatin is dissolved. Stir in sherbet until smooth.
2. Chill until partially set (watch carefully). Fold in oranges, pineapple and bananas. Pour into an oiled 6-cup mold. Chill until salad is firm.
1 piece: 161 cal., 1g fat (0 sat. fat), 2mg chol., 55mg sod., 39g carb. (35g sugars, 1g fiber), 2g pro.

COMFORTING CARROT CASSEROLE

Creamy cheese and crunchy chips add an unusual taste to this easy-to-prepare dish.
—Caroline Hoyt, Scranton, IA

Prep: 15 min. • **Bake:** 20 min.
Makes: 8 servings

- 4 cups sliced fresh carrots
- 1 cup cubed Velveeta
- 2 Tbsp. dried minced onion
- ¼ cup butter, melted
- 1 cup crushed potato chips

1. Place 1 in. of water in a large saucepan; add carrots. Bring to a boil. Reduce heat; cover and simmer for 7-9 minutes or until crisp-tender. Drain.
2. Place carrots in a greased shallow 2-qt. baking dish. Top with cheese and onion. Drizzle with butter; sprinkle with crushed potato chips.
3. Cover and bake casserole at 350° for 20-25 minutes or until bubbly.
½ cup: 164 cal., 12g fat (7g sat. fat), 29mg chol., 311mg sod., 12g carb. (4g sugars, 2g fiber), 4g pro.

SKILLET MAC & CHEESE

CREAM CHEESE MASHED POTATOES

When I serve this easy mash, the bowl is always scraped clean. Before a big feast, I make it early and keep it warm in a slow cooker so I can focus on last-minute details.
—Jill Thomas, Washington, IN

Prep: 20 min. • **Cook:** 15 min.
Makes: 20 servings

- 8 lbs. russet potatoes
- 1 pkg. (8 oz.) cream cheese, softened
- ½ cup butter, melted
- 2 tsp. salt
- ¾ tsp. pepper
  Additional melted butter, optional
- ¼ cup finely chopped green onions

1. Peel and cube potatoes. Place in a large stockpot; add water to cover. Bring to a boil. Reduce heat; cook, uncovered, until tender, 12-15 minutes. Drain.
2. With a mixer, beat the softened cream cheese, ½ cup melted butter, salt and pepper until smooth. Add potatoes; beat until light and fluffy. If desired, top with additional melted butter. Sprinkle with green onions.
¾ cup: 185 cal., 9g fat (5g sat. fat), 25mg chol., 318mg sod., 25g carb. (2g sugars, 2g fiber), 3g pro.

⏱ CONTEST-WINNING ZUCCHINI PANCAKES

In place of potato pancakes, try these cute rounds that are very simple to prepare with on-hand ingredients. They are not only tasty but they're pretty, too.
—Teressa Eastman, El Dorado, KS

Takes: 30 min. • **Makes:** 5 servings

- ⅓ cup biscuit/baking mix
- ¼ cup grated Parmesan cheese
- ⅛ tsp. pepper
- 2 eggs, lightly beaten
- 2 cups shredded zucchini
- 2 Tbsp. butter

1. In a large bowl, combine the biscuit mix, cheese, pepper and eggs just until blended. Add the zucchini and mix well.
2. In a large skillet, melt butter. Drop batter by about ⅓ cupfuls into skillet; press lightly to flatten. Fry until golden brown, about 3 minutes on each side.
1 serving: 128 cal., 9g fat (5g sat. fat), 100mg chol., 248mg sod., 7g carb. (1g sugars, 1g fiber), 5g pro.

⏱ SKILLET MAC & CHEESE

This creamy mac 'n' cheese is so simple it's almost too easy! Kids really go for the rich cheese flavor, but I've never met an adult who didn't love it just as much.
—Ann Bowers, Rockport, TX

Takes: 25 min. • **Makes:** 8 servings

- 2 cups uncooked elbow macaroni (about 8 oz.)
- 2 Tbsp. butter
- 2 Tbsp. all-purpose flour
- 1½ cups half-and-half cream
- ¾ lb. Velveeta, cubed
  Optional toppings: fresh arugula, halved cherry tomatoes and coarsely ground pepper

1. Cook macaroni according to package directions; drain.
2. Meanwhile, in a large cast-iron or other heavy skillet, melt butter over medium heat. Stir in flour until smooth; gradually whisk in cream. Bring to a boil, stirring constantly. Cook and stir until thickened, about 2 minutes. Reduce heat; stir in the cheese until melted.
3. Add macaroni; cook and stir until heated through. Top as desired.
¾ cup: 300 cal., 19g fat (12g sat. fat), 72mg chol., 593mg sod., 20g carb. (5g sugars, 0 fiber), 12g pro.

HOMEMADE FRY BREAD

Crispy, doughy and totally delicious, this fry bread is fantastic with nearly any sweet or savory toppings you can think of. We love it with a little butter, a drizzle of honey and a squeeze of lemon.
—Thelma Tyler, Dragoon, AZ

Prep: 20 min. + standing • **Cook:** 15 min.
Makes: 12 servings

- 2 cups unbleached flour
- ½ cup nonfat dry milk powder
- 3 tsp. baking powder
- ½ tsp. salt
- 4½ tsp. shortening
- ⅔ to ¾ cup water
  Oil for deep-fat frying
  Butter, honey and lemon juice, optional

1. Combine flour, dry milk powder, baking powder and salt; cut in shortening until crumbly. Add water gradually, mixing to form a firm ball. Divide dough; shape into 12 balls. Let stand, covered, for 10 minutes. Roll each ball into a 6-in. circle. With a sharp knife, cut a ½-in.-diameter hole in center of each.

2. In a large cast-iron skillet, heat oil over medium-high heat. Fry the dough circles, 1 at a time, until puffed and golden, about 1 minute on each side. Drain the bread on paper towels; if desired, serve warm with butter, honey and fresh lemon juice.

1 piece: 124 cal., 5g fat (1g sat. fat), 1mg chol., 234mg sod., 17g carb. (2g sugars, 1g fiber), 3g pro.

⏱ CITRUS AVOCADO SPINACH SALAD

Tossing this salad together with creamy avocado and tangy citrus is so easy, and you don't even need to peel the oranges.
—Karole Friemann, Kimberling City, MO

Takes: 15 min. • **Makes:** 8 servings

- 8 cups fresh baby spinach (about 6 oz.)
- 3 cups refrigerated citrus salad, drained
- 2 medium ripe avocados, peeled and sliced
- 1 cup crumbled blue cheese
  Sliced almonds, toasted, optional
  Salad dressing of your choice, optional

Divide spinach among 8 plates; top with citrus salad and avocados. Sprinkle with blue cheese and, if desired, dressing and almonds. Serve immediately.

Note: To toast nuts, bake in a shallow pan in a 350° oven for 5-10 minutes or cook in a skillet over low heat until lightly browned, stirring occasionally.

1 serving: 168 cal., 10g fat (4g sat. fat), 13mg chol., 231mg sod., 16g carb. (10g sugars, 3g fiber), 5g pro.

HOMEMADE
FRY BREAD

SOUPS & SANDWICHES

SWEET & SPICY PINEAPPLE
CHICKEN SANDWICHES P.51

1

2

3

4

5

DISCOVER A PERFECT PAIRING OF TASTY
LUNCHTIME STAPLES, EACH PREPARED
WITH FIVE INGREDIENTS OR FEWER.

SPRING
PEA SOUP

SPRING PEA SOUP

Truly a soup for the pea lover, this recipe originated with an idea in an old cookbook about eating better to live longer. Sauteed potatoes add body to an easy soup with a good texture and superb pea flavor.
—Denise Patterson, Bainbridge, OH

Prep: 10 min. • **Cook:** 30 min.
Makes: 6 servings (1½ qt.)

- 2 cups cubed peeled potatoes
- 2 Tbsp. butter
- 6 cups chicken broth
- 2 cups fresh or frozen peas, thawed
- 2 Tbsp. minced chives
  Microgreens, optional

1. In a large saucepan, saute potatoes in butter until lightly browned. Stir in broth; bring to a boil. Reduce heat; cover and simmer until the potatoes are tender, 10-15 minutes. Add peas; cook until peas are tender, 5-8 minutes. Cool slightly.
2. In a blender, process soup in batches until smooth. Return all to the pan; heat through. Sprinkle with the chives and, if desired, microgreens.
1 cup: 133 cal., 5g fat (2g sat. fat), 15mg chol., 1012mg sod., 18g carb. (4g sugars, 3g fiber), 5g pro.

⏱ SWEET & SPICY PEANUT BUTTER-BACON SANDWICHES

I craved peanut butter and bacon toast while pregnant. Then I sampled a friend's peanut butter with chile pepper in it and loved it. The little zip made the sandwich better.
—Carolyn Eskew, Dayton, OH

Takes: 10 min. • **Makes:** 2 servings

- ¼ cup peanut butter
- 4 slices cinnamon-raisin bread
- ⅛ tsp. cayenne pepper
- 4 crisp cooked bacon strips
- 2 tsp. honey

Spread peanut butter on 2 bread slices; sprinkle with cayenne. Top with bacon strips and drizzle with honey. Top with remaining bread.
1 sandwich: 461 cal., 26g fat (6g sat. fat), 23mg chol., 664mg sod., 43g carb. (15g sugars, 6g fiber), 21g pro.

PULLED PORK SANDWICHES

❄ PULLED PORK SANDWICHES

Foolproof and wonderfully delicious describes my barbecue pork recipe. Just four ingredients and a slow cooker make a fabulous dish with little effort.
—Sarah Johnson, Chicago, IL

Prep: 15 min. • **Cook:** 7 hours
Makes: 6 servings

- 1 Hormel lemon-garlic pork loin filet (about 1⅓ lbs.)
- 1 can (12 oz.) Dr Pepper
- 1 bottle (18 oz.) barbecue sauce
- 6 hamburger buns, split

1. Place pork in a 3-qt. slow cooker. Pour Dr Pepper over top. Cover and cook on low until meat is tender, 7-9 hours.
2. Remove meat; cool slightly. Discard cooking juices. Shred meat with 2 forks; return to slow cooker. Stir in barbecue sauce; heat through. Serve on buns.
Freeze option: Place individual portions of the cooled meat mixture and juice in freezer containers. To use, partially thaw in the refrigerator overnight. Microwave, covered, on high in a microwave-safe dish until heated through, stirring occasionally; add a little water if necessary.
1 sandwich: 348 cal., 8g fat (2g sat. fat), 45mg chol., 1695mg sod., 43g carb. (22g sugars, 2g fiber), 25g pro.

⏱ GRANDMA'S TOMATO SOUP

This recipe is my grandmother's. Originally, Gram even made the tomato juice in it from scratch! Gram had this soup cooking on the stove every time I visited her. She enjoyed making this tomato soup and other favorite dishes for family and friends, and she made everything with love.
—Gerri Sysun, Narragansett, RI

Takes: 15 min. • **Makes:** 2 servings

- 2 Tbsp. butter
- 1 Tbsp. all-purpose flour
- 2 cups tomato juice
- ½ cup water
- 2 Tbsp. sugar
- ⅛ tsp. salt
- ¾ cup cooked wide egg noodles
  Chopped fresh parsley, optional

In a saucepan over medium heat, melt butter. Add flour; stir to form a smooth paste. Gradually add tomato juice and water, stirring constantly; bring to a boil. Cook; stir until thickened, about 2 minutes. Add sugar and salt. Stir in egg noodles and heat through. If desired, sprinkle with parsley.
1 cup: 259 cal., 12g fat (7g sat. fat), 44mg chol., 1144mg sod., 36g carb. (20g sugars, 1g fiber), 4g pro.

🕐 CHEESY WILD RICE SOUP

We often eat easy-to-make soups when we don't have a lot of time to cook. I replaced the wild rice in the original recipe with a boxed rice mix. This creamy concoction is now a family favorite.
—Lisa Hofer, Hitchcock, SD

Takes: 30 min. • **Makes:** 8 servings

- 1 pkg. (6.2 oz.) fast-cooking long grain and wild rice mix
- 4 cups 2% milk
- 1 can (10¾ oz.) condensed cream of potato soup, undiluted
- 8 oz. Velveeta, cubed
- ½ lb. bacon strips, cooked and crumbled
  Optional: Minced chives and oyster crackers

In a large saucepan, prepare the rice mix according to package directions. Add the milk, soup and cheese. Cook and stir until cheese is melted. Garnish with bacon and, if desired, chives and oyster crackers.
1 cup: 464 cal., 29g fat (14g sat. fat), 70mg chol., 1492mg sod., 29g carb. (9g sugars, 1g fiber), 21g pro.

🕐 ITALIAN GRILLED CHEESE SANDWICHES

I made up this recipe for the students in the foods and nutrition class I teach. The kids like it so much, they often go home and fix it for their families.
—Beth Hiott, York, SC

Takes: 25 min. • **Makes:** 4 servings

- 8 slices Italian bread
- 4 Tbsp. prepared pesto
- 4 slices provolone cheese
- 4 slices part-skim mozzarella cheese
- 5 tsp. olive oil
  Marinara sauce warmed, optional

1. Spread 4 bread slices with pesto. Layer with cheeses; top with remaining bread. Spread outsides of sandwiches with oil.
2. In a large skillet over medium heat, toast sandwiches for 3-4 minutes on each side or until the cheese is melted. Serve with marinara if desired.
1 sandwich: 445 cal., 27g fat (10g sat. fat), 35mg chol., 759mg sod., 32g carb. (1g sugars, 2g fiber), 20g pro.

🕐 PESTO HAMBURGERS

Give an Italian twist to basic burgers by topping them with pesto, roasted red peppers strips and mozzarella cheese.
—*Taste of Home* Test Kitchen

Takes: 20 min. • **Makes:** 4 servings

- 1½ lbs. ground beef
- ⅛ tsp. salt
- ⅛ tsp. pepper
- 4 slices part-skim mozzarella cheese
- ½ cup prepared pesto
- ⅓ cup roasted sweet red pepper strips
- 4 hamburger buns, split and toasted

1. Shape beef into four ¾-in.-thick patties. Season with salt and pepper. In a large skillet, cook patties over medium heat until the meat is no longer pink, about 5 minutes on each side.
2. Top each burger with a slice of cheese, 2 Tbsp. pesto and pepper strips. Reduce heat; cover and simmer until cheese is melted, about 2 minutes. Serve on buns.
1 serving: 716 cal., 45g fat (17g sat. fat), 161mg chol., 779mg sod., 25g carb. (3g sugars, 2g fiber), 51g pro

CHEESY WILD RICE SOUP

GREEN CHILE POSOLE

This recipe combines parts of my nanny's and my mother's recipes that they taught to me when I was young. An optional sprinkling of queso fresco on top is an absolute delight, in my opinion.
—Jaime Love, Las Vegas, NV

- -

Prep: 10 min. • **Cook:** 4 hours
Makes: 6 servings

- 1   pork tenderloin (1 lb.), cut into 1-in. pieces
- 2   cans (15 oz. each) hominy, rinsed and drained
- 1   can (4 oz.) chopped green chiles
- ¼   tsp. salt
- ¼   tsp. pepper
- 4   cups chicken broth, divided
- 3   tomatillos, husked and chopped
     Optional: Sliced avocado, lime wedge, sliced jalapenos, sliced radishes, chopped cilantro and sour cream

1. Place first 5 ingredients and 3¾ cups broth in a 3- or 4-qt. slow cooker. Puree the tomatillos with remaining broth in a blender; stir into pork mixture.
2. Cook, covered, on low until the pork is tender, 4-5 hours. If desired, serve with avocado and other toppings.
1⅓ cups: 173 cal., 3g fat (1g sat. fat), 46mg chol., 1457mg sod., 17g carb. (1g sugars, 4g fiber), 17g pro.

🕐 TOMATO SANDWICHES

Use garden-fresh tomatoes for this sandwich. It's simple, but what a summertime treat!
—*Taste of Home* Test Kitchen

- -

Takes: 5 min. • **Makes:** 4 servings

- 8   slices white bread, toasted if desired
- ½   cup mayonnaise, divided
- 2   large ripe tomatoes, sliced ½ in. thick
- ¼   tsp. salt
- ¼   tsp. pepper

Spread 4 slices of bread with half of the mayonnaise. Top with tomatoes; season with salt and pepper. Spread remaining mayonnaise over remaining bread; close the sandwiches.
1 sandwich: 351 cal., 22g fat (3g sat. fat), 10mg chol., 576mg sod., 32g carb. (6g sugars, 3g fiber), 6g pro.

SWEET & SPICY PINEAPPLE CHICKEN SANDWICHES

❄ SWEET & SPICY PINEAPPLE CHICKEN SANDWICHES

My kids often ask for chicken sloppy joes, and this version has a bonus of sweet pineapple. It is a perfect recipe to double for a potluck. Try topping the sandwiches with smoked Gouda cheese.
—Nancy Heishman, Las Vegas, NV

- -

Prep: 15 min. • **Cook:** 2¾ hours
Makes: 8 servings

- 2½ lbs. boneless skinless chicken breasts
- 1   bottle (18 oz.) sweet and spicy barbecue sauce, divided
- 2   Tbsp. honey mustard
- 1   can (8 oz.) unsweetened crushed pineapple, undrained
- 8   hamburger buns, split and toasted
     Optional: Bibb lettuce leaves and thinly sliced red onion

1. Place chicken breasts in a 4-qt. slow cooker. Combine ¼ cup barbecue sauce and mustard; pour over chicken. Cover and cook on low 2½-3 hours or until chicken is tender.
2. Remove chicken; discard liquid. Shred the chicken with 2 forks; return to slow cooker. Add the crushed pineapple and remaining barbecue sauce; cover and cook on high for 15 minutes.
3. Serve on toasted buns with lettuce and onion if desired.
Freeze option: Place the shredded chicken in freezer containers. Cool and freeze. To use, partially thaw in refrigerator overnight. Heat through in a covered saucepan, stirring gently; add broth if necessary.
1 sandwich: 415 cal., 6g fat (1g sat. fat), 78mg chol., 973mg sod., 56g carb. (30g sugars, 2g fiber), 34g pro.

TEST KITCHEN TIP
If your family likes more heat, add a jalapeno pepper.

EASY BUTTERNUT SQUASH SOUP

GOURMET BARBECUE BEEF SANDWICHES

These beef sandwiches were a tradition in my family on winter vacations after a long day of snow skiing, but they're a hit anytime we make them. Serving the barbecue beef on croissants with melty provolone cheese makes the sandwiches a little more special.
—Katie Anderson, Vancouver, WA

Prep: 10 min. • **Cook:** 8 hours 5 min.
Makes: 12 servings

- 1 beef rump roast or bottom round roast (3 to 4 lbs.)
- ½ tsp. salt
- ¼ tsp. pepper
- 1 cup barbecue sauce
- 12 croissants, split
- 12 slices provolone cheese
  Optional ingredients: Tomato slices, lettuce leaves and red onion slices

1. Rub roast with salt and pepper. Place in a 5- or 6-qt. slow cooker. Cook, covered, on low 8-10 hours or until meat is tender.
2. Remove roast; cool slightly. Skim fat from cooking juices. Slice beef; return beef and cooking juices to slow cooker. Add the barbecue sauce; heat through. Place the croissant bottoms on a baking sheet; top with cheese. Broil 4-6 in. from heat until cheese is melted, 1-2 minutes. Top with the beef; if desired, serve with optional toppings. Replace croissant tops.
1 sandwich: 511 cal., 25g fat (13g sat. fat), 125mg chol., 805mg sod., 38g carb. (15g sugars, 2g fiber), 33g pro.

TEST KITCHEN TIP
Mix and match toppings for different takes on this slow-cooked sandwich. Try pepper jack cheese with french-fried onions or sharp cheddar with slaw.

EASY BUTTERNUT SQUASH SOUP

When the weather turns cold, get cozy with a bowl of this butternut squash soup. The cream adds richness, but if you're looking to cut calories, it can be omitted.
—*Taste of Home* Test Kitchen

Takes: 30 min.
Makes: 9 servings (2¼ qt.)

- 1 Tbsp. olive oil
- 1 large onion, chopped
- 3 garlic cloves, minced
- 1 medium butternut squash (3 lbs.), peeled and cubed
- 4 cups vegetable broth
- ¾ tsp. salt
- ¼ tsp. pepper
- ½ cup heavy whipping cream
  Optional: Additional heavy whipping cream and crispy sage leaves

1. In a large saucepan, heat oil over medium heat. Add onion; cook and stir until tender. Add garlic; cook for 1 minute longer.
2. Stir in squash, broth, salt and pepper; bring to a boil. Reduce the heat; simmer, covered, 10-15 minutes or until squash is tender. Puree soup using an immersion blender. Or cool slightly and puree soup in batches in a blender; return to pan. Add cream; cook and stir until heated through. If desired, garnish with additional heavy whipping cream and crispy sage.
1 cup: 157 cal., 7g fat (4g sat. fat), 17mg chol., 483mg sod., 23g carb. (6g sugars, 6g fiber), 3g pro.

GOURMET BARBECUE
BEEF SANDWICHES

BUFFALO CHICKEN SLIDERS

PIGS IN A BLANKET

These baked hot dog sandwiches appeal to kids of all ages. Even my husband, Allan, admits to enjoying every bite! We like to dip them in a bit of ketchup and mustard.
—Linda Young, Longmont, CO

Takes: 25 min. • **Makes:** 4 servings

- 1 tube (8 oz.) refrigerated crescent rolls
- 8 hot dogs
- 1 large egg, lightly beaten
- 1 Tbsp. water
  Caraway seeds

1. Preheat oven to 375°. Separate crescent dough into triangles. Place the hot dogs at wide ends of triangles and roll up. Place on an ungreased baking sheet. Combine egg and water; brush over rolls. Sprinkle the caraway over tops; press lightly into rolls.
2. Bake sandwiches for 12-15 minutes or until golden brown.
2 sandwiches: 516 cal, 39g fat (12g sat. fat), 97mg chol., 1365mg sod., 27g carb. (8g sugars, 0 fiber), 16g pro.

GARLIC BREAD PIZZA SANDWICHES

I love coming up with new ways to make grilled cheese sandwiches for my kids. This version tastes like a classic pizza. Using frozen garlic bread is a timesaver.
—Courtney Stultz, Weir, KS

Takes: 20 min. • **Makes:** 4 servings

- 1 pkg. (11¼ oz.) frozen garlic Texas toast
- ¼ cup pasta sauce
- 4 slices provolone cheese
- 16 slices pepperoni
- 8 slices thinly sliced hard salami
  Additional pasta sauce, warmed, optional

1. Preheat griddle over medium-low heat. Add garlic toast; cook until lightly browned, 3-4 minutes per side.
2. Spoon 1 Tbsp. pasta sauce over each of 4 pieces of toast. Top with the cheese, pepperoni, salami and remaining toast. Cook until crisp and cheese is melted, 3-5 minutes, turning as necessary. If desired, serve with additional sauce.
1 sandwich: 456 cal., 28g fat (10g sat. fat), 50mg chol., 1177mg sod., 36g carb. (4g sugars, 2g fiber), 19g pro.

❋ BUFFALO CHICKEN SLIDERS

I came up with the idea for these sliders from my parents, who'd made a similar recipe for a family get-together. To make it extra special, I sometimes use several different styles of buffalo sauce and let guests mix and match their favorites.
—Christina Addison, Blanchester, OH

Prep: 20 min. • **Cook:** 3 hours
Makes: 6 servings

- 1 lb. boneless skinless chicken breasts
- 2 Tbsp. plus ⅓ cup Louisiana-style hot sauce, divided
- ¼ tsp. pepper
- ¼ cup butter, cubed
- ¼ cup honey
- 12 Hawaiian sweet rolls, warmed
  Optional ingredients: Lettuce leaves, sliced tomato, thinly sliced red onion and crumbled blue cheese

1. Place chicken in a 3-qt. slow cooker. Toss with 2 Tbsp. hot sauce and pepper; cook, covered, on low for 3-4 hours or until tender.
2. Remove chicken; discard cooking juices. In a small saucepan, combine the butter, honey and remaining hot sauce; cook and stir over medium heat until blended. Shred chicken with 2 forks; stir into sauce and heat through. Serve on rolls with desired optional ingredients.
Freeze option: Freeze cooled chicken mixture in freezer containers. To use, partially thaw in refrigerator overnight. Microwave chicken, covered, on high in a microwave-safe dish until heated through, stirring occasionally; add water or broth if necessary.
2 sliders: 396 cal., 15g fat (8g sat. fat), 92mg chol., 873mg sod., 44g carb. (24g sugars, 2g fiber), 24g pro.

ASIAN RAMEN SHRIMP SOUP

A package of store-bought ramen noodles speeds up assembly of this colorful broth with shrimp and carrots. My mother passed the recipe on to me. It's delicious and so quick to fix.
—Donna Hellinger, Lorain, OH

Takes: 15 min. • **Makes:** 4 servings

3½ cups water
1 pkg. (3 oz.) soy sauce ramen noodles
1 cup cooked small shrimp, peeled and deveined
½ cup chopped green onions
1 medium carrot, julienned
2 Tbsp. soy sauce

1. In a large saucepan, bring water to a boil. Set aside seasoning packet from noodles. Add noodles to boiling water; cook and stir for 3 minutes.
2. Add shrimp, onions, carrot, soy sauce and contents of seasoning packet. Cook until heated through, 3-4 minutes longer.
1 cup: 148 cal., 4g fat (2g sat. fat), 83mg chol., 857mg sod., 17g carb. (2g sugars, 1g fiber), 12g pro. **Diabetic exchanges:** 1 starch, 1 lean meat.

ASIAN RAMEN SHRIMP SOUP

HAWAIIAN SAUSAGE SUBS

If you are looking for a different way to use kielbasa, the sweet and mildly spicy flavor of these subs is a nice change of pace.
—Judy Dames, Bridgeville, PA

Prep: 15 min. • **Cook:** 3 hours
Makes: 12 sandwiches

3 lbs. smoked kielbasa or Polish sausage, cut into 3-in. pieces
2 bottles (12 oz. each) chili sauce
1 can (20 oz.) pineapple tidbits, undrained
¼ cup packed brown sugar
12 hoagie buns, split
Thinly sliced green onions, optional

Place the kielbasa in a 3-qt. slow cooker. Combine the chili sauce, pineapple and brown sugar; pour over kielbasa. Cover and cook on low until heated through, 3-4 hours. Serve on buns. If desired, top with green onions.
1 sandwich: 663 cal., 35g fat (12g sat. fat), 76mg chol., 2532mg sod., 64g carb. (27g sugars, 1g fiber), 23g pro.`

TEST KITCHEN TIP
Wow the crowd at the next potluck or tailgate when you wrap these sausage subs individually in foil. Transport them in an insulated cooler so they'll stay warm.

GRANDMA'S
PRESSURE-COOKER
CHICKEN NOODLE SOUP

GRANDMA'S PRESSURE-COOKER CHICKEN NOODLE SOUP

I've made this soup weekly ever since I modified my grandma's recipe for the pressure cooker. Chicken soup, especially this one, is quick to make and budget-friendly for any large family.
—Tammy Stanko, Greensburg, PA

Prep: 10 min. • **Cook:** 25 min. + releasing
Makes: 4 servings

- 2 tsp. olive oil
- 4 bone-in chicken thighs
- 2 medium carrots, peeled, sliced into ½-in. pieces
- 1½ celery ribs, sliced into ½-in. pieces
- 6 cups reduced-sodium chicken broth
- ½ tsp. salt
- ⅛ tsp. pepper
- ½ pkg. (8 oz.) uncooked fine egg noodles, cooked
  Chopped fresh parsley, optional

1. Select saute setting on a 3- or 6-qt. electric pressure cooker and adjust for medium heat; add oil. Brown the chicken thighs. Press cancel. Add carrots, celery and broth to pressure cooker. Lock lid; close pressure-release valve. Adjust to pressure-cook on high for 10 minutes. Allow the pressure to release naturally for 10 minutes, then quick-release any remaining pressure.
2. Stir in salt and pepper. Evenly divide noodles among 4 serving bowls; top each bowl with 1 chicken thigh and top with broth. If desired, sprinkle with parsley.
2 cups soup with 1 chicken thigh: 389 cal., 29g fat (5g sat. fat), 112mg chol., 1262mg sod., 25g carb. (4g sugars, 2g fiber), 31g pro.

READER REVIEW
"Love this soup. I have always made it using the same ingredients. So delicious!"
—SUEMAONE, TASTEOFHOME.COM

CHIPOTLE POMEGRANATE PULLED PORK

CHIPOTLE POMEGRANATE PULLED PORK

Once I was making pulled pork and wanted to kick it up a bit. Pomegranate jelly and smoky chipotles were the perfect addition.
—Tatiana Hendricks, Visalia, CA

Prep: 10 min. • **Cook:** 8½ hours
Makes: 10 servings

- 1 boneless pork shoulder butt roast (3 lbs.)
- 2 Tbsp. steak seasoning
- ½ cup water
- 1 half-pint jar pomegranate jelly or 1 cup red currant jelly
- 3 Tbsp. minced chipotle peppers in adobo sauce
- 10 kaiser rolls, split
  Deli coleslaw, optional

1. Cut roast in half. Place in a 5-qt. slow cooker; sprinkle with steak seasoning. Add water. Cover and cook on low for 8-10 hours or until meat is tender.
2. In a small saucepan, combine jelly and peppers. Cook over medium heat for 5 minutes or until heated through. Remove meat from slow cooker; discard cooking liquid. Shred pork with 2 forks. Return to the slow cooker; top with the jelly mixture. Cover and cook on low for 30 minutes or until heated through. Spoon about ⅔ cup meat onto each roll. If desired, top with coleslaw.
1 sandwich: 616 cal., 28g fat (10g sat. fat), 117mg chol., 839mg sod., 51g carb. (21g sugars, 1g fiber), 37g pro.

❄ WHITE BEAN & CHICKEN CHILI

To create this yummy white chili, I adapted three different recipes. It's mild, so everyone can dig in. People who judge give it ribbons in recipes contests.
—Julie White, Yacolt, WA

Takes: 20 min. • **Makes:** 6 servings

- 3 cans (15 oz. each) cannellini beans, undrained
- 1 can (4 oz.) chopped green chiles
- 3 tsp. chicken bouillon granules
- 3 tsp. ground cumin
- 2 cups water
- 3 cups cubed cooked chicken or turkey
  Minced fresh cilantro, optional

1. In a large saucepan, combine the first 5 ingredients; bring to a boil. Reduce heat; simmer, uncovered, 2-3 minutes to allow flavors to blend, stirring occasionally.
2. Stir in chicken; heat through. If desired, sprinkle with cilantro.
Freeze option: Freeze the cooled chili in freezer containers. To use, partially thaw in refrigerator overnight. Heat through in a saucepan, stirring occasionally and adding a little water if necessary.
1 cup: 323 cal., 6g fat (1g sat. fat), 63mg chol., 1113mg sod., 34g carb. (3g sugars, 10g fiber), 34g pro.

GUMBO IN A JIFFY

This is a yummy dish. My husband loves the kick that the sausage gives this quick gumbo, and it's such a cinch to assemble.
—Amy Flack, Homer City, PA

Takes: 20 min.
Makes: 6 servings (1½ qt.)

- 1 pkg. (12 oz.) smoked sausage, sliced
- 1 can (14½ oz.) diced tomatoes with green peppers and onions, undrained
- 1 can (14½ oz.) chicken broth
- ½ cup water
- 1 cup uncooked instant rice
- 1 can (7 oz.) whole kernel corn, drained
   Sliced green onions, optional

In a large saucepan, cook sliced sausage until browned on both sides. Stir in the tomatoes, broth and water; bring to a boil. Stir in rice and corn; cover and remove from the heat. Let stand for 5 minutes. If desired, top with sliced green onions.

1 cup: 279 cal., 16g fat (7g sat. fat), 40mg chol., 1197mg sod., 22g carb. (6g sugars, 2g fiber), 11g pro.

READER REVIEW
"This was a super easy recipe with a lot of flavor. We made it in our youth cooking class to celebrate a chapter about the Louisiana Purchase. I would make it again."
—JGA2595176, TASTEOFHOME.COM

HAM & CHEESE POCKETS

These unique sandwich pockets are filled with ingredients most kids like.
—Callie Myers, Rockport, TX

Prep: 15 min. + rising • **Bake:** 15 min.
Makes: 10 servings

- 1 loaf (1 lb.) frozen bread dough, thawed
- 2½ cups finely chopped fully cooked ham
- 1 cup shredded Swiss cheese
- 1 large egg yolk
- 1 Tbsp. water

1. Let the dough rise according to package directions. Punch dough down; divide into 10 pieces. On a lightly floured surface, roll each piece into a 5-in. circle.
2. Preheat oven to 375°. Place 1 circle on a greased baking sheet; top with about ¼ cup ham and 2 Tbsp. cheese to within ½ in. of edge. Press the filling to flatten. Combine the egg yolk and water; brush edges of dough. Fold dough over filling and pinch the edges to seal. Repeat with remaining dough and filling. Brush tops with remaining egg yolk mixture.
3. Bake until golden brown, 15-20 minutes. Serve warm or cold.

1 pocket: 229 cal., 9g fat (3g sat. fat), 50mg chol., 729mg sod., 25g carb. (2g sugars, 1g fiber), 14g pro.

GUMBO IN A JIFFY`

**SAUSAGE &
SPINACH CALZONES**

SAUSAGE & PEPPER SHEET-PAN SANDWICHES

Sausage with peppers was always on the table when I was growing up. Here's how to do it the easy way: Just grab a sheet pan and the ingredients, then let the oven do the work.
—Debbie Glasscock, Conway, AR

- -

Prep: 20 min. • **Bake:** 30 min.
Makes: 6 servings

- 1 **lb. uncooked sweet Italian turkey sausage links, roughly chopped**
- 3 **medium sweet red peppers, seeded and sliced**
- 1 **large onion, halved and sliced**
- 1 **Tbsp. olive oil**
- 6 **hot dog buns, split**
- 6 **slices provolone cheese**

1. Preheat the oven to 375°. Place the sausage pieces in a 15x10x1-in. sheet pan, arranging the peppers and onion around sausage. Drizzle olive oil over sausage and vegetables; bake, stirring mixture after 15 minutes, until sausage is no longer pink and vegetables are tender, 30-35 minutes.
2. During the last 5 minutes of baking, arrange buns cut side up in a second sheet pan; top each bun bottom with a cheese slice. Bake until the buns are golden brown and cheese is melted. Spoon sausage and pepper mixture onto bun bottoms. Replace tops.
1 sandwich: 315 cal., 15g fat (5g sat. fat), 43mg chol., 672mg sod., 28g carb. (7g sugars, 2g fiber), 18g pro.

⏱ ❄ SAUSAGE & SPINACH CALZONES

These comforting calzones are perfect for quick meals—or even a midnight snack. My nurse co-workers always ask me to make them when it's my turn to bring in lunch.
—Kourtney Williams, Mechanicsville, VA

- -

Takes: 30 min. • **Makes:** 4 servings

- ½ **lb. bulk Italian sausage**
- 3 **cups fresh baby spinach**
- 1 **tube (13.8 oz.) refrigerated pizza crust**
- ¾ **cup shredded part-skim mozzarella cheese**
- ½ **cup part-skim ricotta cheese**
- ¼ **tsp. pepper**
    Pizza sauce, optional

1. Preheat oven to 400°. In a large skillet, cook and crumble sausage over medium heat until no longer pink, 4-6 minutes; drain. Add spinach; cook and stir until wilted. Remove from heat.
2. On a lightly floured surface, unroll and pat dough into a 15x11-in. rectangle. Cut into 4 rectangles. Sprinkle the mozzarella cheese on half of each rectangle to within 1 in. of edges.
3. Stir the ricotta cheese and pepper into sausage mixture; spoon over mozzarella cheese. Fold the dough over filling; press the edges with a fork to seal. Place on a greased baking sheet.
4. Bake the calzones until light golden brown, 10-15 minutes. If desired, serve with pizza sauce.
Freeze option: Freeze cooled calzones in an airtight freezer container. To use, microwave on high until heated through.
1 calzone: 489 cal., 22g fat (9g sat. fat), 54mg chol., 1242mg sod., 51g carb. (7g sugars, 2g fiber), 23g pro.

MAIN COURSES

**MUFFIN-TIN
LASAGNAS, P. 72**

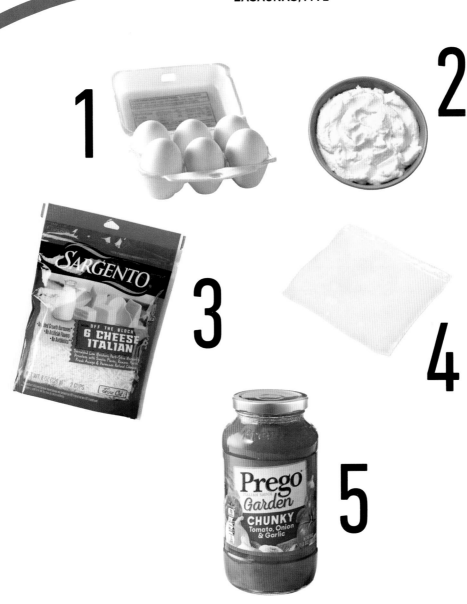

1

2

3

4

5

SAVOR HOME-STYLE FAVORITES, KID-FRIENDLY
DINNERS, HEALTHY SUPPERS AND EVEN DATE-NIGHT
DAZZLERS. ALL ARE READY IN A WINK!

BEEF & RICE
ENCHILADAS

BEEF & RICE ENCHILADAS

With a toddler in the house, I look for foods that are a snap to make. Loaded with beef, cheese and a rice mix, these enchiladas come together without any fuss. They're so good that guests think I spent hours in the kitchen.
—Jennifer Smith, Colona, IL

Prep: 30 min. • **Bake:** 20 min.
Makes: 10 enchiladas

- 1 pkg. (6.8 oz.) Spanish rice and pasta mix
- 1 lb. ground beef
- 2 cans (10 oz. each) enchilada sauce, divided
- 10 flour tortillas (8 in.), warmed
- 1⅔ cups shredded cheddar cheese, divided

1. Prepare rice mix according to package directions. Meanwhile, in a large skillet, cook the beef over medium heat until no longer pink; drain. Stir in the Spanish rice and 1¼ cups enchilada sauce.
2. Spoon about ⅔ cup beef mixture down the center of each tortilla. Top each with 1 Tbsp. cheese; roll up.
3. Place in an ungreased 13x9-in. baking dish. Top with the remaining enchilada sauce and cheese. Bake, uncovered, at 350° until the shredded cheese is melted, 20-25 minutes.
1 enchilada: 415 cal., 17g fat (8g sat. fat), 47mg chol., 1141mg sod., 46g carb. (3g sugars, 3g fiber), 20g pro.

🕑 TOMATO-BASIL PITA PIZZAS

This is one of my favorite warm-weather recipes. It's so easy and so tasty! You can use it as a snack, appetizer or entree and double it to suit your needs.
—Barbra Annino, Galena, IL

Takes: 20 min. • **Makes:** 2 servings

- 2 pita breads (6 in.)
- 2 plum tomatoes, thinly sliced
- 8 fresh basil leaves, thinly sliced
- ¼ cup shredded Asiago cheese
- 2 tsp. olive oil

Place pita breads on an ungreased baking sheet. Layer with the tomatoes, basil and cheese; drizzle with oil. Bake at 350° for 12-14 minutes or until cheese is melted.
1 serving: 269 cal., 9g fat (3g sat. fat), 12mg chol., 362mg sod., 37g carb. (3g sugars, 2g fiber), 10g pro. **Diabetic exchanges:** 2 starch, 1 vegetable, 1 lean meat, 1 fat.

🕑 BEEF STEAKS WITH BLUE CHEESE

I double these juicy steaks when I serve them to company. My guests often ask for the recipe, and they're surprised at how simple it is to make.
—Gloria Nerone, Mentor, OH

Takes: 20 min. • **Makes:** 2 servings

- 2 beef tenderloin steaks (1½ in. thick and 8 oz. each)
- 2 oz. blue cheese, crumbled
- 2 Tbsp. butter, softened
- 2 slices white bread, crusts removed and cut into cubes
- 1 Tbsp. olive oil
- 2 Tbsp. grated Parmesan cheese

1. Place the meat on broiler pan. Broil 4-6 in. from the heat for 5-8 minutes on each side or until meat is browned and cooked to desired doneness (for medium-rare, a thermometer should read 135°; medium, 140°; medium-well, 145°).

2. Meanwhile, in a bowl, combine blue cheese and butter; set aside. In a skillet, saute the bread cubes in oil until golden brown. Sprinkle with Parmesan cheese. Top steaks with blue cheese mixture and sprinkle with croutons; broil 1 minute longer or until cheese is slightly melted.
1 steak: 686 cal., 42g fat (20g sat. fat), 155mg chol., 649mg sod., 16g carb. (2g sugars, 1g fiber), 58g pro.

TEST KITCHEN TIP
Serving size counts when considering nutrition information. An 8-oz. steak is generous, as is the amount of blue cheese topping here. Make this recipe work for you by using 4- or 6-oz. steaks and just half of the topping mixture instead.

⏱ EASY CHICKEN STRIPS

I came up with these crispy strips one night when I was looking for a fast new way to serve chicken. They also make delightful appetizers, especially when served with barbecue or sweet-and-sour sauce.
—Crystal Sheckles-Gibson, Beespring, KY

- -

Takes: 30 min. • **Makes:** 6 servings

- ¼ cup all-purpose flour
- ¾ tsp. seasoned salt
- 1¼ cups crushed cornflakes
- ⅓ cup butter, melted
- 1½ lbs. boneless skinless chicken breasts, cut into 1-in. strips

1. Preheat oven to 400°. In a shallow bowl, combine the flour and seasoned salt. Place cornflakes and butter in separate shallow bowls. Coat the chicken with flour mixture, then dip in butter and coat with cornflakes.
2. Transfer to an ungreased baking sheet. Bake until golden brown and juices run clear, 15-20 minutes.
3 oz. cooked chicken: 283 cal., 12g fat (7g sat. fat), 87mg chol., 438mg sod., 18g carb. (2g sugars, 0 fiber), 25g pro.

⏱ BIG KAHUNA PIZZA

A prebaked pizza crust and refrigerated barbecued pork make this tasty supper idea super-fast and super-easy. Cut into bite-sized pieces, it can also double as a wonderful last-minute appetizer.
—Joni Hilton, Rocklin, CA

- -

Takes: 30 min. • **Makes:** 8 servings

- 1 prebaked 12-in. pizza crust
- 1 carton (16 oz.) refrigerated fully cooked barbecued shredded pork
- 1 can (20 oz.) pineapple chunks, drained
- ⅓ cup chopped red onion
- 2 cups shredded part-skim mozzarella cheese

1. Place the pizza crust on an ungreased 12-in. pizza pan. Spread shredded pork over crust; top with pineapple and onion. Sprinkle with cheese.
2. Bake at 350° for 20-25 minutes or until cheese is melted.
1 piece: 343 cal., 10g fat (4g sat. fat), 33mg chol., 856mg sod., 45g carb. (20g sugars, 2g fiber), 19g pro.

MAPLE PORK RIBS

A luscious maple-mustard sauce will take your next plate of ribs to a new level.
—Phyllis Schmalz, Kansas City, KS

- -

Prep: 10 min. • **Cook:** 5 hours
Makes: 2 servings

- 1 lb. boneless country-style pork ribs, trimmed and cut into 3-in. pieces
- 2 tsp. canola oil
- 1 medium onion, sliced and separated into rings
- 3 Tbsp. maple syrup
- 2 Tbsp. spicy brown or Dijon mustard

In a large skillet, brown ribs in oil on all sides; drain. Place ribs and onion in a 1½-qt. slow cooker. Combine syrup and mustard; pour over ribs. Cover and cook on low until meat is tender, 5-6 hours.
4 oz. cooked pork: 428 cal., 20g fat (6g sat. fat), 98mg chol., 272mg sod., 27g carb. (24g sugars, 2g fiber), 31g pro.

BIG KAHUNA PIZZA

SPECIAL
PORK CHOPS

⏱ GINGER-GLAZED GRILLED SALMON

Our family loves salmon prepared this way, and it's a real treat to make on a summer evening. These fillets may be baked in the oven for 12-14 minutes at 450°, basting occasionally.
—Wanda Toews, Cromer, MB

- -

Takes: 15 min. • **Makes:** 4 servings

- 2 Tbsp. reduced-sodium soy sauce
- 2 Tbsp. maple syrup
- 2 tsp. minced fresh gingerroot
- 2 garlic cloves, minced
- 4 salmon fillets (6 oz. each)

1. For the glaze, mix first 4 ingredients.
2. Place salmon on an oiled grill rack over medium heat, skin side up. Grill, covered, until fish just begins to flake easily with a fork, 4-5 minutes per side; brush top with half of the glaze after turning. Brush with remaining glaze before serving.
1 fillet: 299 cal., 16g fat (3g sat. fat), 85mg chol., 374mg sod., 8g carb. (6g sugars, 0 fiber), 29g pro. **Diabetic exchanges:** 4 lean meat, ½ starch.

⏱ SPECIAL PORK CHOPS

I work nine hours a day, so I need delicious and simple recipes such as this one. My husband thinks I work hard fixing meals, but these chops are easy. In summer, I can make my own salsa and use some to top these chops.
—LaDane Wilson, Alexander City, AL

- -

Takes: 30 min. • **Makes:** 6 servings

- 6 boneless pork chops (6 oz. each)
- 1 Tbsp. canola oil
- 1 jar (16 oz.) salsa

In a large cast-iron or other ovenproof skillet, brown the pork chops in oil; drain any fat. Pour the salsa over chops. Bake, uncovered, at 350° until a thermometer reads 145°, 20-25 minutes. Let stand for 5 minutes.
1 pork chop: 273 cal., 12g fat (4g sat. fat), 82mg chol., 350mg sod., 5g carb. (3g sugars, 0 fiber), 33g pro. **Diabetic exchanges:** 5 lean meat, ½ fat.

SCALLOPS IN SAGE CREAM

TURKEY TENDERLOIN & ROOT VEGGIE SHEET-PAN SUPPER

My family loves turkey tenderloin, so I wanted to try using them in a sheet pan supper. I used potatoes, carrots and onions that I had on hand as well as some bacon. Covering the ingredients with that smoked bacon really made the difference in the finished dish. The vegetables were tender and moist and the turkey was juicy. So quick and easy to prepare .
—Susan Bickta, Kutztown, PA

- -

Prep: 15 min. • **Bake:** 30 min.
Makes: 6 servings

6   bacon strips
2   medium potatoes,
    cut into ½-in. pieces
4   medium carrots, peeled
    and cut into ½-in. pieces
2   medium onions, cut
    into ½-in. pieces
2   tsp. canola oil
1   tsp. salt, divided
½   tsp. pepper, divided
1   pkg. (20 oz.) turkey
    breast tenderloins
    Minced fresh parsley, optional

1. Preheat oven to 375°. Line a 15x10x1-in. baking pan with foil. Place the bacon on prepared pan; bake 15 minutes.
2. Meanwhile, in a large bowl, toss the potatoes, carrots and onions with oil; sprinkle with ½ tsp. salt and ¼ tsp. pepper. Sprinkle remaining salt and pepper on tenderloins.
3. Remove the parcooked bacon from baking pan. Transfer vegetables to pan, spreading evenly. Place tenderloins on top of vegetables; cover with bacon strips. Bake until a thermometer reads 165° and the vegetables are tender, 30-35 minutes. If desired, top with parsley to serve.
3 oz. cooked turkey with ⅔ cup vegetables: 238 cal., 11g fat (3g sat. fat), 42mg chol., 500mg sod., 15g carb. (3g sugars, 2g fiber), 22g pro. **Diabetic exchanges:** 3 lean meat, 1 vegetable, ½ starch.

⏱ SCALLOPS IN SAGE CREAM

I didn't want to hide the ocean freshness of the scallops I bought on the dock from a local fisherman, so I used a few simple ingredients to showcase them.
—Joan Churchill, Dover, NH

- -

Takes: 20 min. • **Makes:** 4 servings

1½ lbs. sea scallops
¼   tsp. salt
⅛   tsp. pepper
3   Tbsp. olive oil, divided
½   cup chopped shallots
¾   cup heavy whipping cream
6   fresh sage leaves, thinly sliced
    Hot cooked pasta, optional

1. Sprinkle scallops with salt and pepper. In a large skillet, cook scallops in 2 Tbsp. oil for 1½ to 2 minutes on each side or until firm and opaque. Remove and keep warm.
2. In the same skillet, saute shallots in remaining oil until tender. Add cream; bring to a boil. Cook and stir 30 seconds or until slightly thickened.
3. Return scallops to the pan; heat through. Stir in sage. Serve with pasta if desired.
1 serving: 408 cal., 28g fat (12g sat. fat), 117mg chol., 441mg sod., 9g carb. (1g sugars, 0 fiber), 30g pro.

BAKED SWISS CHICKEN

Canned soup, white wine, Swiss cheese and crushed croutons dress up chicken breasts in this elegant entree. Ideal for unexpected guests, it only requires a few ingredients.
—Beverly Roberge, Bristol, CT

- -

Prep: 5 min. • **Bake:** 35 min.
Makes: 6 servings

6   boneless skinless chicken
    breast halves (6 oz. each)
1   can (10¾ oz.) condensed cream
    of chicken soup, undiluted
½   cup white wine or chicken broth
6   slices Swiss cheese
1   cup crushed seasoned croutons

1. Preheat oven to 350°. Place chicken in a greased 13x9-in. baking dish. In a small bowl, combine soup and wine; pour over chicken. Top with the cheese and sprinkle with croutons.
2. Bake, uncovered, for 35-40 minutes, or until a thermometer inserted in chicken reads 165°.
1 serving: 308 cal., 13g fat (7g sat. fat), 92mg chol., 614mg sod., 11g carb. (1g sugars, 1g fiber), 31g pro.

TURKEY TENDERLOIN
& ROOT VEGGIE
SHEET-PAN SUPPER

EASY CHICKEN PESTO
STUFFED PEPPERS

✻ SAUCY BAKED CHICKEN

This irresistible chicken gets its wonderful flavor from bubbling in honey and soy sauce while baking. It's always a hit.
—Caroline Champoux, Londonderry, NH

- -

Prep: 25 min. • **Bake:** 30 min.
Makes: 6 servings

- 6   boneless skinless chicken breast halves (6 oz. each)
- 1   cup honey
- ½   cup reduced-sodium soy sauce
- 2   Tbsp. olive oil
- 2   Tbsp. ketchup
- 1   garlic clove, minced
- ¼   tsp. salt
- ⅛   tsp. pepper

1. Preheat oven to 375°. Place chicken in a greased 13x9-in. baking dish. In a small bowl, mix the remaining ingredients; pour over chicken.
2. Bake, uncovered, 30-35 minutes or until thermometer inserted in the chicken reads 165°, basting occasionally. Remove chicken from dish and keep warm.
3. Transfer the sauce to a small saucepan. Bring to a boil; cook and stir 12-15 minutes or until sauce is reduced to 1¼ cups.
Freeze option: Cover and freeze cooled chicken and sauce in freezer containers. To use, partially thaw in the refrigerator overnight. Reheat in a foil-lined 13x9-in. baking dish in a preheated 325° oven until heated through, covering if necessary to prevent excess browning.
1 chicken breast half with about 3 Tbsp. sauce: 412 cal., 8g fat (2g sat. fat), 94mg chol., 1013mg sod., 49g carb. (47g sugars, 0 fiber), 36g pro.

⏱ EASY CHICKEN PESTO STUFFED PEPPERS

On busy weeknights, I don't want to spend more than 30 minutes preparing dinner, nor do I want to wash a towering pile of dishes. This recipe delivers without sacrificing flavor!
—Olivia Cruz, Greenville, SC

- -

Takes: 25 min. • **Makes:** 4 servings

- 4   medium sweet yellow or orange peppers
- 1½   cups shredded rotisserie chicken
- 1½   cups cooked brown rice
- 1   cup prepared pesto
- ½   cup shredded Havarti cheese
    Fresh basil leaves, optional

1. Cut peppers lengthwise in half; remove stems and seeds. Place the peppers on a baking sheet, skin side up. Broil 4 in. from heat until the skins blister, about 5 minutes. Reduce oven temperature to 350°.
2. Meanwhile, in a large bowl, combine the chicken, rice and pesto. When cool enough to handle, fill the peppers with the chicken mixture; return to baking sheet. Bake until heated through, about 5 minutes. Sprinkle with cheese; bake until cheese is melted, 3-5 minutes. If desired, sprinkle with basil.
2 stuffed pepper halves: 521 cal., 31g fat (7g sat. fat), 62mg chol., 865mg sod., 33g carb. (7g sugars, 5g fiber), 25g pro.

DID YOU KNOW?

Common olive oil works better for cooking at high heat than virgin or extra-virgin oil. These higher grades have ideal flavor for cold foods, but they smoke at lower temperatures.

⏱ TORTELLINI WITH SAUSAGE & MASCARPONE

When I crave Italian comfort food on a busy night and don't have a lot of time to cook, this dish is fast and yummy. You can have it on the table in less time than a takeout order.
—Gerry Vance, Millbrae, CA

Takes: 20 min. • **Makes:** 6 servings

- 1 pkg. (20 oz.) refrigerated cheese tortellini
- 8 oz. bulk Italian sausage
- 1 jar (24 oz.) pasta sauce with mushrooms
- ½ cup shredded Parmesan cheese
- 1 carton (8 oz.) mascarpone cheese
   Crushed red pepper flakes, optional

1. Prepare tortellini according to package directions. Meanwhile, in a large cast-iron or other heavy skillet, cook the sausage over medium heat until no longer pink, 6-8 minutes, breaking into crumbles; drain. Stir in pasta sauce; heat through.
2. Drain tortellini, reserving 1 cup cooking water. Add tortellini to sauce and enough reserved cooking water to reach desired consistency; toss to coat. Stir in Parmesan cheese; dollop with mascarpone cheese. If desired, sprinkle with red pepper flakes.
1 cup: 637 cal., 37g fat (17g sat. fat), 113mg chol., 1040mg sod., 57g carb. (11g sugars, 4g fiber), 24g pro.

TORTELLINI WITH SAUSAGE & MASCARPONE

⏱ BEAN BURRITOS

I always have the ingredients for this cheesy bean burrito recipe on hand. Cooking the rice and shredding the cheese the night before save precious minutes at dinnertime.
—Beth Osborne Skinner, Bristol, TN

Takes: 30 min. • **Makes:** 6 servings

- 1 can (16 oz.) refried beans
- 1 cup salsa
- 1 cup cooked long grain rice
- 2 cups shredded cheddar cheese, divided
- 12 flour tortillas (6 in.)
   Shredded lettuce, optional

1. Preheat oven to 375°. In a large bowl, combine the beans, salsa, rice and 1 cup cheese. Spoon about ⅓ cup off-center on each tortilla. Fold the sides and ends over filling and roll up.
2. Arrange burritos in a greased 13x9-in. baking dish. Sprinkle with remaining 1 cup cheese. Cover; bake until heated through, 20-25 minutes. If desired, topped with the shredded lettuce.
2 burritos: 216 cal., 9g fat (4g sat. fat), 23mg chol., 544mg sod., 24g carb. (1g sugars, 3g fiber), 9g pro.

CHEESY BLACK
BEAN NACHOS

🕐 CHEESY BLACK BEAN NACHOS

We're trying to go meatless once a week, and this dish helps make those meals fun, quick and super delicious. It's also a smart way to use up beans and canned tomatoes from your pantry.
—Cynthia Nelson, Saskatoon, SK

Takes: 20 min. • **Makes:** 4 servings

- 1   can (15 oz.) black beans, rinsed and drained
- 1   can (14½ oz.) diced tomatoes, well drained
- 3   to 4 jalapeno peppers, seeded and sliced
- 4   cups multigrain tortilla chips
- 1   cup shredded cheddar cheese
      Optional toppings: Sour cream, chopped fresh cilantro and additional jalapeno slices

1. Preheat oven to 350°. Mix the beans, tomatoes and jalapenos. Arrange chips in an even layer in a 15x10x1-in. pan. Top with bean mixture and cheese.
2. Bake, uncovered, until cheese is melted, 10-12 minutes. Serve immediately with the toppings as desired.
Note: Wear disposable gloves when cutting hot peppers; the oils can burn skin. Avoid touching your face.
1 serving: 371 cal., 17g fat (6g sat. fat), 28mg chol., 672mg sod., 42g carb. (6g sugars, 7g fiber), 15g pro.

TEST KITCHEN TIP
Spreading out the ingredients in a large pan helps the chips stay crunchy and evenly coated with toppings.

CONTEST-WINNING BARBECUED PORK CHOPS

🕐 CONTEST-WINNING BARBECUED PORK CHOPS

Sherry, honey, barbecue and steak sauces combine to give these chops a beautiful glaze and dressed-up flavor. The sauce works well on chicken breasts, too.
—LaJuana Kay Holland, Amarillo, TX

Takes: 20 min. • **Makes:** 6 servings

- ⅓   cup hickory smoke-flavored barbecue sauce
- ⅓   cup A.1. steak sauce
- ⅓   cup sherry or unsweetened apple juice
- 2   Tbsp. honey
- 6   bone-in pork loin chops (¾ in. thick and 8 oz. each)
- ¾   tsp. salt
- ½   tsp. pepper

1. Mix the first 4 ingredients; reserve ⅓ cup sauce for serving.
2. Sprinkle the pork chops with the salt and pepper. Place on an oiled grill rack over medium heat. Grill, covered, until a thermometer reads 145°, 4-6 minutes per side, brushing frequently with remaining sauce after turning. Let stand 5 minutes before serving. Serve pork chops with reserved sauce.
1 pork chop with 2 tsp. sauce: 299 cal., 10g fat (4g sat. fat), 98mg chol., 771mg sod., 16g carb. (14g sugars, 0 fiber), 35g pro.

LEMON-GARLIC SALMON STEAKS

I always enjoy making this easy recipe for my husband, Jim. He loves salmon and garlic, and they go together so well in this recipe.
—Mary Lynn Baronett, Waynesburg, PA

Prep: 10 min. • **Bake:** 25 min.
Makes: 6 servings

- 6 to 8 garlic cloves, minced
- 4 Tbsp. olive oil, divided
- 6 salmon steaks (6 oz. each)
- ⅔ cup lemon juice
- ¼ cup minced fresh parsley
  Salt and pepper to taste

1. Preheat oven to 350°. In a small skillet, saute garlic in 1 Tbsp. oil for 1 minute.
2. Arrange salmon steaks in a greased 13x9-in. baking dish. Combine the lemon juice, parsley, salt, pepper and remaining oil; pour over salmon steaks. Top with the garlic mixture.
3. Bake, uncovered, 25-30 minutes or until fish flakes easily with a fork.

1 steak: 403 cal., 27g fat (5g sat. fat), 100mg chol., 103mg sod., 3g carb. (1g sugars, 0 fiber), 34g pro.

Tarragon Salmon Steaks: Omit garlic and olive oil. Stir 3 Tbsp. melted butter and 3 Tbsp. minced fresh tarragon into lemon juice mixture. Proceed as directed.

🕐 MUFFIN-TIN LASAGNAS

This is a super fun way to serve lasagna and a wonderful way to surprise everyone at the table. Easy and quick, these little cups can be made with whatever ingredients your family likes best.
—Sally Kilkenny, Granger, IA

Takes: 30 min. • **Makes:** 1 dozen

- 1 large egg, lightly beaten
- 1 carton (15 oz.) part-skim ricotta cheese
- 2 cups shredded Italian cheese blend, divided
- 1 Tbsp. olive oil
- 24 wonton wrappers
- 1 jar (24 oz.) garden-style pasta sauce
  Minced fresh parsley, optional

1. Preheat oven to 375°. In a bowl, mix egg, ricotta cheese and 1¼ cups Italian cheese blend.
2. Generously grease 12 muffin cups with the oil; line each with a wonton wrapper. Fill each with 1 Tbsp. ricotta mixture and 1½ Tbsp. pasta sauce. Top each with a second wrapper, rotating corners and pressing down the centers. Repeat the ricotta and sauce layers. Sprinkle with remaining cheese blend.
3. Bake for 20-25 minutes until cheese is melted. If desired, sprinkle with parsley.

2 mini lasagnas: 414 cal., 19g fat (9g sat. fat), 83mg chol., 970mg sod., 36g carb. (8g sugars, 2g fiber), 22g pro.

LEMON-GARLIC
SALMON STEAKS

KALUA PORK

Planning a luau themed party? Then this is the perfect main dish for your get together. It's a no-fuss crowd pleaser meal, and it's easy to clean up! A Hawaiian friend shared this recipe with me while I was stationed in Pearl Harbor several years ago. It feeds a crowd and everyone loves it.
—Becky Friedman, Hammond, LA

- -

Prep: 10 min. • **Cook:** 8 hours
Makes: 18 servings

- 1 boneless pork shoulder roast (5 to 6 lbs.)
- 1 Tbsp. liquid smoke
- 4 tsp. sea salt (preferably Hawaiian Alaea Sea Salt)
  Hot cooked rice, optional

1. Pierce pork with a fork; rub with liquid smoke and salt. Place pork in a 6-qt. slow cooker. Cook, covered, on low until pork is tender, 8-10 hours.
2. Remove roast; shred with 2 forks. Strain the cooking juices; skim fat. Return pork to slow cooker. Stir in enough cooking juices to moisten; heat through. If desired, serve with rice.
Freeze option: Freeze cooled meat mixture and the juices in freezer containers. To use, partially thaw in the refrigerator overnight. Heat meat through in a saucepan, stirring occasionally; add broth if necessary.
3 oz. cooked pork: 205 cal., 13g fat (5g sat. fat), 75mg chol., 504mg sod., 0 carb. (0 sugars, 0 fiber), 21g pro.
Diabetic exchanges: 3 medium-fat meat.

🕑 FAST BAKED FISH

We always have a good supply of fresh fish, so I make this dish often. It's moist, tender and flavorful.
—Judie Anglen, Riverton, WY

- -

Takes: 25 min. • **Makes:** 4 servings

- 1¼ lbs. fish fillets
- 1 tsp. seasoned salt
  Pepper to taste
  Paprika, optional
- 3 Tbsp. butter, melted

1. Preheat oven to 400°. Place fish in a greased 11x7-in. baking dish. Sprinkle with seasoned salt, pepper and paprika if desired. Drizzle with butter.
2. Cover and bake until fish just begins to flake easily with a fork, 15-20 minutes.
1 serving: 270 cal., 17g fat (7g sat. fat), 110mg chol., 540mg sod., 0 carb. (0 sugars, 0 fiber), 28g pro

GRILLED
PINEAPPLE
CHICKEN

GRILLED PINEAPPLE CHICKEN

A trip to Hawaii is easy with this juicy grilled pineapple chicken. Simply give it a quick marinade, fire up the grill and let it sizzle. We love this low-carb recipe!
—Charlotte Rogers, Va Beach, VA

- -

Prep: 10 min. + marinating • **Grill:** 10 min.
Makes: 4 servings

- ¼ cup unsweetened pineapple juice
- 2 Tbsp. sherry
- 2 Tbsp. soy sauce
- ¼ tsp. ground ginger
  Dash salt
  Dash pepper
- 4 boneless skinless chicken breast halves (6 oz. each)
  Grilled pineapple and sliced green onions, optional

1. In a large bowl, combine the first 6 ingredients; add chicken and turn to coat. Cover; refrigerate 1-2 hours.
2. Drain and discard marinade. Grill chicken, covered, over medium heat or broil 4 in. from the heat 5-7 minutes on each side or until a meat thermometer reads 165°. If desired, serve with grilled pineapple and sliced green onions.
1 serving: 187 cal., 4g fat (1g sat. fat), 94mg chol., 209mg sod., 1g carb. (0 sugars, 0 fiber), 35g pro. **Diabetic exchanges:** 5 lean meat.

**SAUSAGE &
SAUERKRAUT**

🕐 SAUSAGE & SAUERKRAUT

*Three young children involved in different
activities keep me running year-round.
I created this for those extra-busy nights.
It delivers flavor—and makes life a little
easier, too.*
—Mary Lyon, Spotsylvania, VA

- -

Takes: 30 min. • **Makes:** 4 servings

- 6 medium red potatoes, cubed
- 2 Tbsp. canola oil
- 1 small onion, halved and sliced
- 1 lb. smoked sausage, cut
     into ¼-in. pieces
- 1 pkg. (16 oz.) sauerkraut,
     rinsed and well drained
- ¼ tsp. pepper

In a large skillet, saute the potatoes in oil
for 5-6 minutes or until lightly browned.
Stir in onion; saute for 3-4 minutes or until
tender. Add the sausage, sauerkraut and
pepper. Cook, uncovered, over medium
heat 4-5 minutes or until heated through,
stirring occasionally.
1½ cups: 567 cal., 38g fat (14g sat. fat),
76mg chol., 2043mg sod., 36g carb.
(7g sugars, 6g fiber), 20g pro.

❄ ROAST BEEF & GRAVY

*This is by far the simplest way to make
roast beef and gravy. On busy days, I can
put this main dish in the slow cooker and
forget about it. My family likes enjoying it
with mashed potatoes and fruit salad.*
—Abby Metzger, Larchwood, IA

- -

Prep: 15 min. • **Cook:** 8 hours
Makes: 10 servings

- 1 boneless beef chuck roast (3 lbs.)
- 2 cans (10¾ oz. each) condensed
     cream of mushroom
     soup, undiluted
- ⅓ cup sherry or beef broth
- 1 envelope onion soup mix

1. Cut the roast in half; place in a 3-qt.
slow cooker. In a large bowl, combine
remaining ingredients; pour over roast.
2. Cover and cook on low for 8-10 hours
or until meat is tender.
Freeze option: Place sliced pot roast in
freezer containers; top with cooking juices.
Cool and freeze. To use, partially thaw in
refrigerator overnight. Heat through in
a covered saucepan, gently stirring and
adding a little water if necessary.
4 oz.-weight: 267 cal., 14g fat (6g sat. fat),
90mg chol., 517mg sod., 4g carb. (0 sugars,
0 fiber), 27g pro.

BAKED HAM
WITH PINEAPPLE

*I first learned the technique for cooking
ham with pineapple for a themed dinner
I hosted. Since it is widely known as the
symbol of hospitality, pineapple was the
star ingredient on our menu and on this
lovely baked ham.*
—JoAnn Fox, Johnson City, TN

- -

Prep: 10 min. • **Bake:** 2 hours
Makes: 20 servings

- 1 fully cooked bone-in
     ham (6 to 8 lbs.)
     Whole cloves
- 1 can (20 oz.) sliced pineapple
- ½ cup packed brown sugar
- 12 maraschino cherries

Place the ham in roasting pan. Score
the surface with shallow diagonal cuts,
making diamond shapes; insert cloves
into diamonds. Cover and bake at 325°
1½ hours. Drain the pineapple, reserving
¼ cup of the juice. Combine brown sugar
and reserved pineapple juice; pour over
ham. Arrange the pineapple and cherries
on ham. Bake, uncovered, 30-45 minutes
longer or until a thermometer reads 140°
and the ham is heated through.
3 oz. cooked ham: 219 cal., 13g fat (5g sat.
fat), 48mg chol., 924mg sod., 8g carb.
(8g sugars, 0 fiber), 17g pro.

🕐 AIR-FRYER
CHICKEN THIGHS

*This air-fryer chicken thighs recipe creates
meat that is crispy on the outside but super
juicy on the inside. The paprika and garlic
seasoning blend comes through beautifully.*
—*Taste of Home* Test Kitchen

- -

Takes: 20 min. • **Makes:** 4 servings

- 4 bone-in chicken thighs
     (about 1½ lbs.)
- 1 Tbsp. olive oil
- ¾ tsp. salt
- ½ tsp. paprika
- ¼ tsp. garlic powder
- ¼ tsp. pepper

Preheat air-fryer to 375°. Brush chicken
with oil. Combine remaining ingredients;
sprinkle over chicken. Place chicken, skin
side up, in a single layer on tray in air-fryer
basket. Cook until a thermometer inserted
in chicken reads 170°-175°, 15-17 minutes.
1 chicken thigh: 255 cal., 18g fat (4g sat. fat),
81mg chol., 511mg sod., 0 carb. (0 sugars,
0 fiber), 23g pro.

BAKED HAM
WITH PINEAPPLE

ARTICHOKE CHICKEN
PESTO PIZZA

POLENTA CHILI CASSEROLE

This delicious vegetarian bake combines spicy chili, mixed veggies and homemade polenta. It's so hearty that no one seems to miss the meat.
—Dan Kelmenson, West Bloomfield, MI

Prep: 20 min. • **Bake:** 35 min. + standing
Makes: 8 servings

    4   cups water
    ½   tsp. salt
    1¼ cups yellow cornmeal
    2   cups shredded cheddar
        cheese, divided
    3   cans (15 oz. each) vegetarian
        chili with beans
    1   pkg. (16 oz.) frozen mixed
        vegetables, thawed
        and well drained

1. Preheat oven to 350°. In a large heavy saucepan, bring water and salt to a boil. Reduce heat to a gentle boil; slowly whisk in cornmeal. Cook and stir with a wooden spoon 15-20 minutes or until polenta is thickened and pulls away cleanly from sides of pan.
2. Remove from the heat. Stir in ¼ cup cheddar cheese until melted.
3. Spread mixture into a 13x9-in. baking dish coated with cooking spray. Bake, uncovered, for 20 minutes. Meanwhile, heat chili according to package directions.
4. Spread the vegetables over polenta; top with chili. Sprinkle with remaining cheese. Bake 12-15 minutes longer or until cheese is melted. Let casserole stand 10 minutes before serving.
1 piece: 297 cal., 7g fat (4g sat. fat), 20mg chol., 556mg sod., 43g carb. (7g sugars, 12g fiber), 19g pro.

READER REVIEW
"This was a success for dinner with everyone—kids and hubby! My hubby even went for seconds. (This doesn't happen too much, as he can be pickier than the kids at times)!"
—EQUESTSARAH81, TASTEOFHOME.COM

ARTICHOKE CHICKEN PESTO PIZZA

Make pizza night an upscale affair with this fun twist on the traditional pie. A prebaked crust and prepared pesto keep things quick and easy.
—Trisha Kruse, Eagle, ID

Takes: 15 min. • **Makes:** 8 slices

    1   prebaked 12-in. pizza crust
    ½   cup prepared pesto
    2   cups cubed cooked chicken breast
    2   jars (6½ oz. each) marinated
        artichoke hearts, drained
    2   cups shredded part-skim
        mozzarella cheese
        Optional: Grated Parmesan cheese
        and minced fresh basil

Preheat oven to 425°. Place crust on an ungreased 12-in. pizza pan. Spread with pesto. Arrange chicken and artichokes over top; sprinkle with cheese. Bake until golden brown, 10-12 minutes. If desired, top with Parmesan cheese and minced fresh basil.
1 piece: 381 cal., 20g fat (6g sat. fat), 45mg chol., 880mg sod., 28g carb. (2g sugars, 4g fiber), 23g pro.

RASPBERRY CHICKEN

Basic skillet-cooked chicken gets a slightly sweet kick with this fresh, fun raspberry sauce, and it's scrumptious over rice, too.
—Anita Hennesy, Hagerstown, MD

Takes: 30 min. • **Makes:** 4 servings

    4   boneless skinless chicken
        breast halves (5 oz. each)
    ¼   tsp. salt
    ¼   tsp. pepper
    ½   cup seedless raspberry jam
    2   Tbsp. balsamic vinegar
    1   Tbsp. reduced-sodium soy sauce
    ⅛   tsp. crushed red pepper flakes

1. Sprinkle chicken with salt and pepper. In a large skillet coated with cooking spray, cook the chicken over medium heat 5-7 minutes on each side or until a thermometer reads 170°.
2. Meanwhile, in a small saucepan, combine the remaining ingredients. Bring to a boil; cook until the liquid is reduced to ½ cup. Serve with chicken.
1 serving: 260 cal., 3g fat (1g sat. fat), 78mg chol., 369mg sod., 28g carb. (25g sugars, 0 fiber), 29g pro. **Diabetic exchanges:** 4 lean meat, 1½ starch.

CAPRESE CHICKEN WITH BACON

Smoky bacon, fresh basil, ripe tomatoes and gooey mozzarella top these appealing chicken breasts. The aroma as the chicken bakes is irresistible!
—Tammy Hayden, Quincy, MI

Prep: 20 min. • **Bake:** 15 min.
Makes: 4 servings

- 8   bacon strips
- 4   boneless skinless chicken breast halves (6 oz. each)
- 1   Tbsp. olive oil
- ½   tsp. salt
- ¼   tsp. pepper
- 2   plum tomatoes, sliced
- 6   fresh basil leaves, thinly sliced
- 4   slices part-skim mozzarella cheese

1. Preheat oven to 400°. Place the bacon in an ungreased 15x10x1-in. baking pan. Bake until partially cooked but not crisp, 8-10 minutes. Remove to paper towels to drain.

2. Place chicken in an ungreased 13x9-in. baking pan; brush with oil and sprinkle with salt and pepper. Top with tomatoes and basil. Wrap each in 2 bacon strips, arranging bacon in a crisscross.

3. Bake, uncovered, until a thermometer reads 165°, 15-20 minutes. Top with the cheese; bake until melted, 1 minute longer.

1 chicken breast half: 373 cal., 18g fat (7g sat. fat), 123mg chol., 821mg sod., 3g carb. (1g sugars, 0 fiber), 47g pro.

CAPRESE CHICKEN WITH BACON

⏱ PARMESAN PORK MEDALLIONS

I was so happy to find this recipe. I have served it countless times for family and friends. It takes very little prep time and adapts easily to serve any number.
—Angela Ciocca, Saltsburg, PA

Takes: 20 min. • **Makes:** 2 servings

- ½   lb. pork tenderloin
- 2   Tbsp. seasoned bread crumbs
- 1   Tbsp. grated Parmesan cheese
- ¼   tsp. salt
      Dash pepper
- 2   tsp. canola oil
- ¼   cup sliced onion
- 1   garlic clove, minced

1. Cut the pork into 4 slices; flatten to ¼-in. thickness. In a large shallow dish, combine the bread crumbs, cheese, salt and pepper. Add pork, 1 slice at a time, and turn to coat.

2. In a large skillet over medium heat, cook pork in oil until meat is no longer pink, 2-3 minutes on each side. Remove and keep warm.

3. Add onion to the pan; cook and stir until tender. Add garlic, cook for 1 minute longer. Serve with pork.

2 pieces: 220 cal., 9g fat (2g sat. fat), 65mg chol., 487mg sod., 8g carb. (1g sugars, 1g fiber), 25g pro. **Diabetic exchanges:** 3 lean meat, 1 fat, ½ starch.

BEST-EVER
LAMB CHOPS

BEST-EVER LAMB CHOPS

My mom just loved a good lamb chop, and this recipe was her favorite way to have them. I've also grilled these chops with fantastic results.
—Kim Mundy, Visalia, CA

- -

Prep: 10 min. + chilling • **Broil:** 10 min.
Makes: 4 servings

- 1 tsp. each dried basil, marjoram and thyme
- ½ tsp. salt
- 8 lamb loin chops (3 oz. each)
  Mint jelly, optional

1. Combine herbs and salt; rub over lamb chops. Cover and refrigerate for 1 hour.
2. Broil lamb chops 4-6 in. from heat for 5-8 minutes on each side or until meat reaches desired doneness (for medium-rare, a thermometer should read 135°; for medium, 140°; for medium-well, 145°). Serve with mint jelly if desired.
2 lamb chops: 157 cal., 7g fat (2g sat. fat), 68mg chol., 355mg sod., 0 carb. (0 sugars, 0 fiber), 22g pro. **Diabetic exchanges:** 3 lean meat.
Honey-Glazed Lamb Chops: Omit step 1, herbs and salt. In a saucepan, heat over medium-low heat, ⅓ cup each honey and prepared mustard and ⅛ tsp. each onion, salt and pepper for 2-3 minutes or until honey is melted. Brush sauce over both sides of lamb. Proceed as directed in step 2.

🕐 SHRIMP PASTA ALFREDO

My son loves any recipe with Alfredo sauce. When he cooked as a bachelor, shrimp pasta was one of his first recipes. Now his children ask for it.
—Gail Lucas, Olive Branch, MS

- -

Takes: 25 min. • **Makes:** 4 servings

- 3 cups uncooked bow tie pasta
- 2 cups frozen peas
- 1 lb. peeled and deveined cooked medium shrimp, tails removed
- 1 jar (15 oz.) Alfredo sauce
- ¼ cup shredded Parmesan cheese

1. In a Dutch oven, cook pasta according to package directions, adding peas during the last 3 minutes of cooking; drain and return to pan.
2. Stir in shrimp and sauce; heat through over medium heat, stirring occasionally. Sprinkle with cheese.
2 cups: 545 cal., 16g fat (9g sat. fat), 206mg chol., 750mg sod., 60g carb. (5g sugars, 6g fiber), 41g pro.

TANGY BEEF
TURNOVERS

🕐 TANGY BEEF TURNOVERS

My mom's recipe for these flavorful pockets called for dough made from scratch, but I streamlined it by using refrigerated crescent rolls.
—Claudia Bodeker, Ash Flat, AR

- -

Takes: 30 min. • **Makes:** 1 dozen

- 1 lb. ground beef
- 1 medium onion, chopped
- 1 jar (16 oz.) sauerkraut, rinsed, drained and chopped
- 1 cup shredded Swiss cheese
- 3 tubes (8 oz. each) refrigerated crescent rolls

1. In a large skillet, cook beef and onion over medium heat until meat is no longer pink; drain. Add sauerkraut and cheese.
2. Unroll the crescent roll dough and separate into rectangles. Place the rectangles on greased baking sheets; pinch the seams to seal. Place ½ cup beef mixture in the center of each rectangle. Bring corners to the center and pinch to seal. Bake at 375° for 15-18 minutes or until golden brown.
2 turnovers: 634 cal., 35g fat (7g sat. fat), 63mg chol., 1426mg sod., 54g carb. (14g sugars, 2g fiber), 27g pro.

🕐 SPICY CHICKEN NUGGETS

We devour these golden brown chicken nuggets at least once a week. If you would prefer to tone down the heat, just skip the chipotle pepper.
—Cheryl Cook, Palmyra, VA

- -

Takes: 30 min. • **Makes:** 6 servings

- 1½ cups panko bread crumbs
- 1½ cups grated Parmesan cheese
- ½ tsp. ground chipotle pepper, optional
- ¼ cup butter, melted
- 1½ lbs. boneless skinless chicken thighs, cut into 1½-in. pieces

1. Preheat oven to 400°. In a shallow bowl, mix bread crumbs, cheese and, if desired, chipotle pepper. Place butter in a separate shallow bowl. Dip chicken pieces in butter, then in the crumb mixture, patting to help coating adhere.
2. Place chicken on a greased 15x10x1-in. baking pan; sprinkle with remaining crumb mixture. Bake for 20-25 minutes or until no longer pink.
1 serving: 371 cal., 22g fat (10g sat. fat), 113mg chol., 527mg sod., 13g carb. (1g sugars, 1g fiber), 29g pro.

COOKIES, BARS, BROWNIES & CANDIES

MAPLE-BACON WHITE CHOCOLATE FUDGE P. 86

1

2

3

4

5

THANKS TO THESE SIMPLE RECIPES, YOU CAN ALWAYS HAVE A LITTLE SOMETHING SWEET ON HAND.

HOMEMADE HOLIDAY
MARSHMALLOWS

HOMEMADE HOLIDAY MARSHMALLOWS

This recipe was my grandpa's favorite. Every Christmastime, he would be busy making marshmallows for his family and friends.
—Diana Byron, New London, OH

- -

Prep: 55 min. + standing
Makes: about 9½ dozen

- 2 tsp. butter
- 3 envelopes unflavored gelatin
- 1 cup cold water, divided
- 2 cups sugar
- 1 cup light corn syrup
- ⅛ tsp. salt
- 1 tsp. clear vanilla extract
  Optional toppings: Melted chocolate, hot fudge and/or caramel ice cream topping
  Optional garnishes: Baking cocoa, confectioners' sugar, crushed assorted candies, chopped nuts, colored sugars and/or sprinkles

1. Line a 13x9-in. pan with foil and grease the foil with butter; set aside.
2. In a large metal bowl, sprinkle the gelatin over ½ cup water; set aside. In a large heavy saucepan, combine sugar, corn syrup, salt and remaining water. Bring to a boil, stirring occasionally. Cook, without stirring, until a candy thermometer reads 240° (soft-ball stage).
3. Remove from the heat and gradually add to gelatin. Beat on high speed until mixture is thick and the volume is doubled, about 15 minutes. Beat in vanilla. Spread into prepared pan. Cover and let stand at room temperature 6 hours or overnight.
4. Using foil, lift marshmallows out of pan. With a knife or pizza cutter coated with cooking spray, cut into 1-in. squares. Dip or drizzle marshmallows with toppings if desired; coat with garnishes as desired. Store in an airtight container in a cool, dry place.
1 serving: 22 cal., 0 fat (0 sat. fat), 0 chol., 5mg sod., 6g carb. (4g sugars, 0 fiber), 0 pro.

READER REVIEW

"These were fantastic! My son loves marshmallows, so this was our Christmas project this year. They were super simple to make, and my boys had a blast decorating them. We will definitely be doing this again."
—HCHAMBERS, TASTEOFHOME.COM

CHERRY CRUMB DESSERT BARS

CHERRY CRUMB DESSERT BARS

Here's a sweet treat that's especially good with a dollop of whipped cream or a scoop of ice cream! The crumb topping has a wonderful nutty flavor, and no one will guess this streusel started with a handy cake mix.
—Ann Eastman, Santa Monica, CA

- -

Prep: 15 min. • **Bake:** 30 min.
Makes: 16 servings

- ½ cup cold butter
- 1 pkg. yellow cake mix (regular size)
- 1 can (21 oz.) cherry or blueberry pie filling
- ½ cup chopped walnuts

1. In a large bowl, cut butter into cake mix until crumbly. Set aside 1 cup for topping. Pat remaining crumbs onto the bottom and ½ in. up the sides of a greased 13x9-in. baking pan.
2. Spread pie filling over crust. Combine walnuts with reserved crumbs; sprinkle over top. Bake at 350° for 30-35 minutes or until golden brown. Cut into bars.
1 piece: 294 cal., 11g fat (5g sat. fat), 15mg chol., 290mg sod., 46g carb. (26g sugars, 2g fiber), 3g pro.

ORANGE CRISPIES

Add a little sunshine to your cookie jar with this recipe. When I want to spread cheer, I'll bake up a double batch to give out.
—Ruth Gladstone, Brunswick, MD

Prep: 15 min. • **Bake:** 10 min./batch
Makes: 3½ dozen

- 1 cup shortening
- 1 cup sugar
- 1 large egg, room temperature
- 1½ tsp. orange extract
- ½ tsp. salt
- 1½ cups all-purpose flour
  Additional sugar or orange-colored sugar

1. In a small bowl, cream shortening and sugar until light and fluffy, 5-7 minutes. Beat in the egg, extract and salt. Add flour; mix well. Drop dough in rounded tablespoonfuls 2 in. apart onto ungreased baking sheets.
2. Bake at 375° until edges begin to brown, about 10 minutes. Cool for 1-2 minutes; remove from pans to wire racks. Sprinkle warm cookies with sugar.
2 cookies: 158 cal., 9g fat (2g sat. fat), 10mg chol., 59mg sod., 16g carb. (9g sugars, 0 fiber), 1g pro.

PEANUT BUTTER CANDY

During the holidays, I make a lot of candy for friends, and this simple recipe seems to be a favorite. The white chocolate and peanut butter make a perfect blend.
—Deloris Morrow, Lake City, IA

Prep: 10 min. + cooling
Makes: about 1½ lbs.

- ½ tsp. butter
- 1¼ lbs. white candy coating, coarsely chopped
- 1½ cups chunky peanut butter

1. Line a 9-in. square pan with foil; butter the foil with ½ tsp. butter and set aside.
2. In a microwave-safe bowl, melt candy coating; stir until smooth. Stir in peanut butter until melted. Transfer to prepared pan. Cool to room temperature. Cut into squares.
1 piece: 331 cal., 22g fat (11g sat. fat), 0 chol., 118mg sod., 30g carb. (26g sugars, 2g fiber), 6g pro.

SOUTH DAKOTA FRITO TREATS

Yep, they're made with corn chips! These salty sweets were a staple after meetings at the quilt guild I belonged to in South Dakota.
—Carol Tramp, Wynot, NE

Prep: 15 min. + standing • **Makes:** 2 dozen

- 2 pkg. (9¾ oz. each) corn chips, divided
- 2 cups semisweet chocolate chips, divided
- 1 cup sugar
- 1 cup light corn syrup
- 1 cup creamy peanut butter

1. Spread 1 package of corn chips on the bottom of a greased 13x9-in. baking pan; sprinkle with 1 cup chocolate chips.
2. In a large heavy saucepan, combine sugar and corn syrup. Bring to a boil; cook and stir 1 minute. Remove from heat; stir in peanut butter. Pour half of the peanut butter mixture over chip mixture. Top with remaining corn chips and chocolate chips; drizzle with the remaining peanut butter mixture. Let stand until set. Cut into bars.
1 bar: 337 cal., 18g fat (5g sat. fat), 0 chol., 196mg sod., 43g carb. (29g sugars, 2g fiber), 5g pro.

LEMON SNOWFLAKES

You'll need just four items to whip up these delightful cookies. Confectioners' sugar highlights the cracked tops to give them their snowflake appearance.
—Linda Barry, Dianna, TX

Prep: 30 min. • **Bake:** 10 min./batch
Makes: 5½ dozen

- 1 pkg. lemon cake mix (regular size)
- 2¼ cups whipped topping
- 1 large egg, room temperature
  Confectioners' sugar

1. In a large bowl, combine cake mix, whipped topping and egg until well blended. Batter will be very sticky.
2. Drop batter by teaspoonfuls into the confectioners' sugar; roll lightly to coat. Place on ungreased baking sheets. Bake at 350° for 10-12 minutes or until lightly browned and tops are cracked. Remove to wire racks to cool.
1 cookie: 37 cal., 1g fat (1g sat. fat), 3mg chol., 59mg sod., 7g carb. (4g sugars, 0 fiber), 0 pro.

ORANGE
CRISPIES

**MAPLE-BACON WHITE
CHOCOLATE FUDGE**

PEANUT BUTTER CHOCOLATE BARS

These chewy peanut butter chocolate bars are the perfect no-fuss contribution to a potluck or bake sale. I've discovered that the trick is to get them into the refrigerator to set up before they disappear!
—Lorri Speer, Centralia, WA

- -

Prep: 30 min. + chilling • **Makes:** 2 dozen

1	cup sugar
1	cup light corn syrup
1	cup peanut butter
6	cups crisp rice cereal
2	cups semisweet chocolate chips, melted

In a large saucepan, combine the sugar, corn syrup and peanut butter. Cook and stir over medium-low heat until sugar is dissolved. Remove from heat; stir in the cereal. Spread into a greased 13x9-in. pan and press lightly. Spread the melted chocolate over top; refrigerate until set. Cut into bars.
1 bar: 302 cal., 14g fat (6g sat. fat), 0 chol., 96mg sod., 46g carb. (37g sugars, 2g fiber), 4g pro.

TEST KITCHEN TIP

If you're a total chocolate lover, swap in chocolate-flavored crisp rice cereal as an alternative to the traditional flavor.

❄ MAPLE-BACON WHITE CHOCOLATE FUDGE

Bored with the same old fudge? Prepare it with white chips, add maple flavoring and load it up with bacon. Then be prepared to share the recipe!
—Mindie Hilton, Susanville, CA

- -

Prep: 10 min. + chilling
Makes: about 2½ lbs. (81 pieces)

1	tsp. plus ¼ cup butter, cubed, divided
10	slices ready-to-serve fully cooked bacon
2	pkg. (10 to 12 oz. each) white baking chips
1	can (14 oz.) sweetened condensed milk
¾	tsp. maple flavoring

1. Line a 9-in. square pan with foil; grease foil with 1 tsp. butter. Heat bacon according to package directions. Crumble bacon and set aside.

2. In a microwave-safe bowl, combine baking chips, condensed milk, flavoring and remaining butter. Microwave on high 1 minute; stir until smooth. (If chips aren't completely melted, microwave in 10- to 20-second intervals until melted; stir until smooth.) Stir in bacon; pour into prepared pan. Refrigerate, covered, for 2 hours or until firm.

3. Using foil, lift fudge out of pan. Remove foil; cut fudge into 1-in. squares.
To make ahead: Store fudge, layered between waxed paper, in an airtight container in the refrigerator. Serve at room temperature.
Freeze option: Wrap fudge in waxed paper, then in foil. Place in freezer containers and freeze. To thaw, bring wrapped fudge to room temperature.
1 piece: 62 cal., 4g fat (2g sat. fat), 5mg chol., 26mg sod., 7g carb. (7g sugars, 0 fiber), 1g pro.

**PEANUT BUTTER
CHOCOLATE BARS**

POTATO
CHIP BITES

❄ POTATO CHIP BITES

A friend at church gave me the recipe for these buttery, light and crisp cookies. It's never failed to bring me compliments.
—Brenda Stone, Sterrett, AL

Prep: 15 min. + chilling
Bake: 10 min. + cooling
Makes: about 3 dozen

  2 cups butter, softened
1¼ cups sugar
  3 tsp. vanilla extract
3½ cups all-purpose flour
2⅓ cups crushed potato chips
  2 cups semisweet chocolate chips, optional
     Additional crushed potato chips, optional

1. In a large bowl, cream softened butter and sugar until light and fluffy, 5-7 minutes. Beat in vanilla extract. In another bowl, whisk flour and crushed potato chips; gradually beat into the creamed mixture.
2. Divide dough in half; shape each into a 10-in.-long roll. Wrap and refrigerate 1 hour or until firm.
3. Preheat oven to 350°. Unwrap and cut dough crosswise into ½-in. slices. Place 1 in. apart on ungreased baking sheets. Bake 10-12 minutes or until bottoms are light brown. Cool on pans for 2 minutes. Remove to wire racks to cool completely. If desired, melt chocolate chips; dip each cookie halfway into chocolate; allow the excess to drip off. Place on waxed paper. If desired, sprinkle cookies with additional crushed potato chips.
Freeze option: Place the wrapped logs in an airtight container; freeze. To use, unwrap frozen logs and cut into slices. If necessary, let dough stand 15 minutes at room temperature before cutting. Bake as directed.
1 cookie: 164 cal., 10g fat (6g sat. fat), 24mg chol., 93mg sod., 16g carb. (6g sugars, 0 fiber), 1g pro.

TOFFEE TURTLE SQUARES

TOFFEE TURTLE SQUARES

Here's an easy way to make turtle candy for a big group. These bars are very rich, so a little square will do ya.
—Glenna Tooman, Boise, ID

Prep: 15 min. • **Bake:** 15 min. + cooling
Makes: 4 dozen

  2 cups all-purpose flour
1½ cups packed brown sugar, divided
  1 cup plus 3 Tbsp. softened butter, divided
1½ cups coarsely chopped pecans
1½ cups semisweet chocolate chips

1. Preheat oven to 350°. Line a 13x9-in. baking pan with parchment, letting ends extend up sides.
2. Beat flour, 1 cup brown sugar and ½ cup butter until well blended (the mixture will be dry and crumbly). Firmly press into the prepared pan. Sprinkle chopped pecans over flour mixture.
3. In a small saucepan, combine the remaining brown sugar and remaining butter. Bring to a boil over medium heat. Boil until the sugar is dissolved, stirring constantly, about 1 minute. Carefully pour mixture over pecans. Bake until bubbly and edges start to brown, 15-20 minutes.
4. Remove from the oven. Immediately sprinkle with chocolate chips. Let stand until chocolate begins to melt; spread evenly. Cool completely in pan on a wire rack. Lifting with parchment, remove from pan. Cut into squares.
1 bar: 134 cal., 9g fat (4g sat. fat), 12mg chol., 39mg sod., 15g carb. (10g sugars, 1g fiber), 1g pro.

PEANUT BUTTER CLUSTERS

Four ingredients and 20 minutes make for one fabulous treat! This chocolate-coated crunch also freezes well, so try keeping some on hand.
—Pat Maxwell, Taft, CA

- -

Prep: 20 min. + chilling
Makes: about 3½ dozen

2 cups peanut butter chips
1 cup milk chocolate chips
1½ cups dry roasted peanuts
1 cup crushed ridged potato chips

In a microwave-safe bowl, melt peanut butter chips and chocolate chips; stir until smooth. Stir in peanuts and potato chips. Drop by level tablespoonfuls onto waxed paper-lined baking sheets. Refrigerate until firm. Store in an airtight container.
1 piece: 96 cal., 6g fat (2g sat. fat), 1mg chol., 70mg sod., 8g carb. (5g sugars, 1g fiber), 3g pro.

⏱ NO-BAKE CEREAL BARS

With crisp rice cereal and peanut butter, these bars taste almost like candy.
—Pauline Christiansen, Columbus, KS

- -

Takes: 20 min. • **Makes:** about 10 dozen

2 cups sugar
2 cups corn syrup
1 jar (40 oz.) chunky peanut butter
6 cups Cheerios oat cereal
6 cups Chex crisp rice cereal

In a large saucepan, cook and stir sugar and corn syrup until the sugar is dissolved. Remove from the heat. Add peanut butter; mix well. Stir in cereals. Spread quickly into 2 lightly greased 15x10x1-in. pans. Cut into bars while warm.
1 serving: 95 cal., 5g fat (1g sat. fat), 0 chol., 79mg sod., 12g carb. (7g sugars, 1g fiber), 3g pro.

DID YOU KNOW?
Corn syrup is an invert sugar, meaning it is liquid in its natural state. This quality helps it stop sugar crystals from forming in frostings, candies and other sweet recipes.

VANILLA MERINGUE COOKIES

These sweet little swirls are light as can be. They're all you need after a big dinner.
—Jenni Sharp, Milwaukee, WI

- -

Prep: 20 min.
Bake: 40 min. + standing
Makes: about 5 dozen

3 large egg whites
1½ tsp. clear or regular vanilla extract
¼ tsp. cream of tartar
Dash salt
⅔ cup sugar

1. Place egg whites in a small bowl; let stand at room temperature 30 minutes.
2. Preheat oven to 250°. Add the vanilla, cream of tartar and salt to egg whites; beat on medium speed until foamy. Gradually add sugar, 1 Tbsp. at a time, beating on high after each addition, until sugar is dissolved. Continue beating until stiff glossy peaks form, about 7 minutes.

3. Cut a small hole in the tip of a pastry bag or in a corner of a food-safe plastic bag; insert a #32 star tip. Transfer the meringue to bag. Pipe 1¼-in.-diameter cookies 2 in. apart onto parchment-lined baking sheets.
4. Bake for 40-45 minutes or until firm to the touch. Turn off oven; leave meringues in oven 1 hour (leave oven door closed). Remove from oven; cool completely on baking sheets. Remove meringues from paper; store in an airtight container at room temperature.
1 cookie: 10 cal., 0 fat (0 sat. fat), 0 chol., 5mg sod., 2g carb. (2g sugars, 0 fiber), 0 pro.
Diabetic exchanges: 1 free food.

MAGIC
BROWNIE
BARS

CHOCOLATY S'MORES BARS

One night, my husband had some friends over to play poker, and he requested these s'mores bars. They polished off the pan and asked for more! I shared the recipe, and now their families make them, too.
—Rebecca Shipp, Beebe, AR

- -

Prep: 15 min. + cooling • **Makes:** 1½ dozen

- ¼ cup butter, cubed
- 1 pkg. (10 oz.) large marshmallows
- 1 pkg. (12 oz.) Golden Grahams cereal
- ⅓ cup milk chocolate chips, melted

1. In a large saucepan, melt butter over low heat. Add marshmallows; cook and stir until blended. Remove from heat. Stir in cereal until coated.
2. Press into a greased 13x9-in. pan using a buttered spatula. Drizzle with melted chocolate. Cool completely before cutting. Store in an airtight container.
1 bar: 159 cal., 4g fat (2g sat. fat), 7mg chol., 197mg sod., 30g carb. (17g sugars, 1g fiber), 1g pro.

MAGIC BROWNIE BARS

One of my all-time favorite treats as a kid was magic cookie bars. This recipe combines all the same classic flavors in a brownie!
—Mandy Rivers, Lexington, SC

- -

Prep: 15 min. • **Bake:** 35 min. + cooling
Makes: 3 dozen

- 1 pkg. (17½ oz.) brownie mix
- 1 pkg. (11 oz.) butterscotch chips
- 2 cups sweetened shredded coconut
- 1 cup chopped pecans, optional
- 1 can (14 oz.) sweetened condensed milk

1. Preheat oven to 350°. Line a 13x9-in. baking pan with foil, letting ends extend up sides; grease foil.
2. Prepare brownie mix batter according to package directions. Transfer to prepared pan. Top with butterscotch chips, coconut and, if desired, pecans. Drizzle with milk. Bake for 35-40 minutes or until topping is light golden.
3. Cool completely in pan on a wire rack. Lifting with foil, remove brownies from pan. Cut into bars. Store the bars in an airtight container.
1 bar: 200 cal., 10g fat (5g sat. fat), 14mg chol., 91mg sod., 25g carb. (21g sugars, 1g fiber), 3g pro.

CHOCOLATE-CARAMEL
TRUFFLES

CHOCOLATE-CARAMEL TRUFFLES

These candies disappear as fast as I can make them. The five-ingredient microwave recipe is easy and super fun to make. When drizzled with white chocolate and packaged with ribbon, they're a pretty gift.
—Charlotte Midthun, Granite Falls, MN

Prep: 1 hour + chilling • **Makes:** 2½ dozen

- 26 caramels
- 1 cup milk chocolate chips
- ¼ cup heavy whipping cream
- 1⅓ cups semisweet chocolate chips
- 1 Tbsp. shortening

1. Line an 8-in. square dish with plastic wrap; set aside. In a microwave-safe bowl, combine caramels, milk chocolate chips and cream. Microwave, uncovered, on high 1 minute; stir. Microwave 1 minute longer, stirring every 15 seconds or until the caramels are melted and mixture is smooth. Spread into the prepared dish; refrigerate for 1 hour or until firm.
2. Using plastic wrap, lift candy out of pan. Cut into 30 pieces; roll each piece into a 1-in. ball. Cover and refrigerate for 1 hour or until firm.
3. In a microwave-safe bowl, melt the semi-sweet chips and shortening; stir until smooth. Dip caramels in chocolate; allow excess to drip off. Place on waxed paper; let stand until set. If desired, use additional melted chocolate to drizzle over truffles. Refrigerate until firm.
Note: This recipe was tested in a 1,100-watt microwave.
1 truffle: 110 cal., 6g fat (3g sat. fat), 4mg chol., 27mg sod., 15g carb. (13g sugars, 1g fiber), 1g pro.

READER REVIEW
"These are easy to make, and they taste delicious! They make a very nice gift for friends and loved ones. Welcome in a new neighbor, thank teachers and bus drivers, bring to an expectant mother or acknowledge your co-workers. Any chocolate lover will be thrilled to receive these."
—CHRISTINE, TASTEOFHOME.COM

BIRTHDAY CAKE FUDGE

BIRTHDAY CAKE FUDGE

This decadent treat is the perfect thing to make your birthday special. Or prepare it ahead and package it as a surprise gift for a friend.
—Rashanda Cobbins, Milwaukee, WI

Prep: 10 min. + chilling
Makes: 64 servings

- 1 can (14 oz.) sweetened condensed milk
- 1½ cups white baking chips
- 3 Tbsp. butter
- ⅛ tsp. salt
- 1½ cups unprepared funfetti cake mix
- 3 Tbsp. sprinkles

1. Line an 8-in. square pan with foil or parchment; grease foil lightly. In a large heavy saucepan, cook and stir the milk, baking chips, butter and salt over low heat until smooth. Remove from heat; stir in cake mix until dissolved. Spread into prepared pan; top with sprinkles. Refrigerate, covered, until firm, about 2 hours.
2. Using foil, lift fudge out of pan. Remove foil; cut fudge into 1-in. squares. Store in an airtight container in the refrigerator.
1 piece: 59 cal., 2g fat (2g sat. fat), 4mg chol., 47mg sod., 9g carb. (7g sugars, 0 fiber), 1g pro.

PEANUT BUTTER COOKIE CUPS

PEANUT BUTTER COOKIE CUPS

I'm a busy schoolteacher and pastor's wife. I wouldn't dare show my face at a church dinner or bake sale without these tempting peanut butter treats. They're quick, easy to make and always a hit.
—Kristi Tackett, Banner, KY

Prep: 35 min. • **Bake:** 15 min.
Makes: 3 dozen

- 1 pkg. (17½ oz.) peanut butter cookie mix
- 36 miniature peanut butter cups, unwrapped

1. Preheat oven to 350°. Prepare cookie mix according to package directions. Roll the dough into 1-in. balls. Place in greased miniature muffin cups. Press dough evenly onto bottom and up sides of each cup.
2. Bake for 11-13 minutes or until set. Immediately place a peanut butter cup in each cup; press down gently. Cool 10 minutes; carefully remove from pans.
1 serving: 119 cal., 7g fat (2g sat. fat), 6mg chol., 89mg sod., 13g carb. (3g sugars, 1g fiber), 2g pro

❄ POLKA-DOT MACAROONS

Macaroons studded with M&M's are easy to mix up in a hurry. That's good, because believe me, they never last long.
—Janice Lass, Dorr, MI

Prep: 15 min.
Bake: 10 min./batch + cooling
Makes: about 4½ dozen

- 5 cups sweetened shredded coconut
- 1 can (14 oz.) sweetened condensed milk
- ½ cup all-purpose flour
- 1½ cups M&M's minis

1. Preheat oven to 350°. In a large bowl, mix coconut, milk and flour until blended; stir in M&M's.
2. Drop the macaroon mixture by rounded tablespoonfuls 2 in. apart onto greased baking sheets. Bake 8-10 minutes or until edges are lightly browned. Remove from pans to wire racks to cool.
Freeze option: Freeze the macaroons, layered between waxed paper, in freezer containers. To use, thaw before serving.
1 cookie: 99 cal., 5g fat (4g sat. fat), 3mg chol., 31mg sod., 13g carb. (10g sugars, 1g fiber), 1g pro.

RASPBERRY ALMOND STRIPS

RASPBERRY ALMOND STRIPS

A cup of tea is the perfect complement to these scrumptious cookie strips dressed up with raspberry filling. Chopped almonds make them an extra-special treat.
—Taste of Home Test Kitchen

Prep: 20 min. • **Bake:** 15 min./batch
Makes: 32 cookies

- 1 tube (16½ oz.) refrigerated sugar cookie dough, softened
- ⅔ cup all-purpose flour
- ½ cup finely chopped almonds
- 6 Tbsp. raspberry cake and pastry filling

1. Preheat oven to 350°. In a bowl, beat cookie dough, flour and almonds until blended. Divide dough in half. Roll each half into a 13½x2-in. rectangle on an ungreased baking sheet.
2. Using a wooden spoon handle, make a ¼-in.-deep indentation lengthwise down the center of each rectangle. Bake for 5 minutes.
3. Spoon raspberry filling into indentation. Bake 8-10 minutes longer or until cookie is golden brown. Cool on pans 2 minutes.
4. Remove from pans to a cutting board; cut each rectangle crosswise into 16 slices. Transfer to wire racks to cool.
1 cookie: 106 cal., 4g fat (1g sat. fat), 2mg chol., 55mg sod., 16g carb. (9g sugars, 1g fiber), 1g pro.

TIGER BUTTER FUDGE

My younger brother and I share a passion for candymaking. This smooth and creamy fudge from a co-worker of mine features the classic combination of peanut butter and chocolate.
—Peg Kipp, Lewisburg, PA

Prep: 25 min. + chilling • **Makes:** 2½ lbs.

- 1½ tsp. butter, softened
- 2⅔ cups vanilla or white chips
- 2⅔ cups milk chocolate chips
- 1 cup creamy peanut butter, divided
- 2 Tbsp. shortening, divided

1. Line a 9-in. square pan with foil and grease the foil with butter; set aside. In a heavy saucepan, melt the vanilla chips, ½ cup peanut butter and 1 Tbsp. shortening over low heat; cook and stir constantly until smooth. Pour into the prepared pan.
2. In another heavy saucepan, melt milk chocolate chips, ½ cup peanut butter and 1 Tbsp. shortening over low heat; cook and stir constantly until smooth. Drizzle over vanilla layer. Swirl with a knife. Refrigerate for 30 minutes or until firm. Using the foil, lift fudge out of pan. Gently peel off the foil; cut into 1-in. squares.
1 piece: 82 cal., 5g fat (3g sat. fat), 3mg chol., 23mg sod., 7g carb. (6g sugars, 0 fiber), 1g pro.

CAKES, PIES & OTHER DESSERTS

**RAINBOW SHERBET
ANGEL FOOD CAKE P.101**

1

2

3

4

5

GOOD TIMES ARE MADE SWEETER WHEN YOU
SERVE UP ONE OF THESE SO-EASY SPECIALTIES.

APPLE PIE
A LA MODE

APPLE PIE A LA MODE

I was planning a dinner party, and wanted a dessert that wowed. My caramel apple ice cream pie certainly does the trick. Now it's a family favorite.
—Trisha Kruse, Eagle, ID

- -

Prep: 15 min. + freezing
Makes: 8 servings

- 1 can (21 oz.) apple pie filling
- 1 graham cracker crust (9 in.)
- 2 cups butter pecan ice cream, softened if necessary
- 1 jar (12 oz.) hot caramel ice cream topping
- ¼ cup chopped pecans, toasted

1. Spread half of the pie filling over crust. Top with half of the butter pecan ice cream; freeze for 30 minutes. Drizzle with half of the caramel topping; layer with remaining pie filling. Freeze for 30 minutes. Scoop the remaining ice cream over top. Freeze, covered, until firm.
2. Remove from freezer 30 minutes before serving. In a microwave, warm remaining caramel topping. Serve the pie with warm caramel topping; sprinkle with pecans.
Note: To toast nuts, bake in a shallow pan in a 350° oven for 5-10 minutes or cook in a skillet over low heat until lightly browned, stirring occasionally.
1 piece: 398 cal., 14g fat (4g sat. fat), 13mg chol., 357mg sod., 69g carb. (59g sugars, 2g fiber), 3g pro.

TEST KITCHEN TIP

To toast pecans, spread them in a single layer on a baking sheet lined with parchment paper; bake in a 350° oven until golden brown, about 6-10 minutes depending on how finely the nuts are chopped. Open the oven and stir often.

BERRY DREAM CAKE

BERRY DREAM CAKE

I use cherry gelatin to give a boxed cake mix an eye-appealing marbled effect. It's super festive-looking. Top it with any fruit you like!
—Margaret McNeil, Germantown, TN

- -

Prep: 15 min. + chilling
Bake: 30 min. + chilling
Makes: 15 servings

- 1 pkg. white cake mix (regular size)
- 1½ cups boiling water
- 1 pkg. (3 oz.) cherry gelatin
- 1 pkg. (8 oz.) cream cheese, softened
- 2 cups whipped topping
- 4 cups fresh strawberries, coarsely chopped

1. Prepare and bake the cake mix batter according to package directions, using a greased 13x9-in. baking pan.
2. In a small bowl, add the boiling water to gelatin; stir 2 minutes to completely dissolve. Cool cake on a wire rack for 3-5 minutes. Using a wooden skewer, pierce holes in top of cake to within 1 in. of edge, twisting skewer gently to make slightly larger holes. Gradually pour the gelatin over cake, being careful to fill each hole. Cool 15 minutes. Refrigerate, covered, 30 minutes.
3. In a large bowl, beat cream cheese until fluffy. Fold in whipped topping. Carefully spread over cake. Top with strawberries. Cover and refrigerate for at least 2 hours before serving.
1 piece: 306 cal., 16g fat (6g sat. fat), 54mg chol., 315mg sod., 37g carb. (22g sugars, 1g fiber), 5g pro.

BLOOD ORANGE CARAMEL TARTE TATIN

Blood orange season is pretty short, so I use them in everything I possibly can. Whenever I have something to go to, my friends demand that I bring this dessert.
—Pamela Butkowski, Hermosa Beach, CA

- -

Prep: 20 min. • **Bake:** 20 min. + cooling
Makes: 6 servings

½   cup butter, cubed
½   cup packed brown sugar
1   tsp. vanilla extract
1   medium blood orange, thinly sliced
1   sheet frozen puff pastry, thawed
     Vanilla ice cream, optional

1. Preheat the oven to 400°. In an 8-in. cast-iron or other ovenproof skillet, melt butter over medium heat; stir in the brown sugar and vanilla until dissolved. Arrange the orange slices in a single layer over brown sugar.
2. On a lightly floured surface, unfold the puff pastry. Roll to a 9-in. square; place over oranges, tucking in corners.
3. Bake until tart is golden brown and filling is heated through, 20-25 minutes. Cool 10 minutes before inverting onto a serving plate. Serve warm, with ice cream if desired.
1 piece: 416 cal., 26g fat (12g sat. fat), 41mg chol., 262mg sod., 43g carb. (19g sugars, 3g fiber), 3g pro.

🕐 CHOCOLATE MOLTEN CAKES

Be prepared to swoon once you dip into this indulgent flourless cake and warm chocolate oozes from its center.
—Matthew Lawrence, Vashon, WA

- -

Takes: 30 min. • **Makes:** 6 servings

2   tsp. plus 1 cup butter, cubed, divided
6   tsp. plus ¼ cup sugar, divided
1¼ lbs. semisweet chocolate, chopped
2   large eggs, room temperature
6   large egg yolks, room temperature

1. Preheat oven to 350°. Grease six 6-oz. ramekins or custard cups with 2 tsp. butter. Sprinkle sides and bottoms of each ramekin with 1 tsp. sugar; set aside.
2. In a double boiler or metal bowl over hot water, melt chocolate and remaining butter; stir until smooth. Remove from heat. In a large bowl, beat the eggs, egg yolks and remaining sugar until thick and lemon-colored. With a spatula, fold half of the egg mixture into chocolate mixture just until blended. Fold in the remaining egg mixture.
3. Transfer to prepared ramekins. Place ramekins on a baking sheet. Bake for 17-20 minutes or until a thermometer inserted in the center reads 160° and sides of cakes are set.
4. Remove from the oven; let stand for 1 minute. Run a knife around sides of ramekins; invert onto dessert plates. Serve immediately.
1 serving: 877 cal., 68g fat (39g sat. fat), 359mg chol., 255mg sod., 67g carb. (60g sugars, 7g fiber), 12g pro.

🕐 CHERRY CREAM CHEESE TARTS

It's hard to believe that just five ingredients and a few minutes of preparation can result in these delicate and scrumptious tarts!
—Cindi Mitchell, Waring, TX

- -

Takes: 10 min. • **Makes:** 2 servings

3   oz. cream cheese, softened
¼   cup confectioners' sugar
⅛   to ¼ tsp. almond or vanilla extract
2   individual graham cracker shells
¼   cup cherry pie filling

In a small bowl, beat cream cheese, sugar and extract until smooth. Spoon into the graham cracker shells. Top with pie filling. Refrigerate until serving.
1 tart: 362 cal., 20g fat (10g sat. fat), 43mg chol., 265mg sod., 42g carb. (29g sugars, 1g fiber), 4g pro.

EASY KEY LIME PIE

You need only five ingredients to create this refreshing pie. It's easy enough to make for a weeknight dessert, but special enough for weekend potlucks.
—*Taste of Home* Test Kitchen

- -

Prep: 20 min. + chilling
Makes: 8 servings

1   pkg. (8 oz.) cream cheese, softened
1   can (14 oz.) sweetened condensed milk
½   cup Key lime juice or lime juice
1   graham cracker crust (9 in.)
2   cups whipped topping
     Lime slices, optional

In a large bowl, beat cream cheese until smooth. Beat in milk and lime juice until blended. Transfer to crust. Refrigerate, covered, at least 4 hours. Just before serving, garnish with whipped topping and, if desired, lime slices.
1 piece: 417 cal., 22g fat (13g sat. fat), 46mg chol., 274mg sod., 48g carb. (42g sugars, 0 fiber), 7g pro.

RAINBOW SHERBET ANGEL FOOD CAKE

Talk about a dessert that pops off the plate! Sometimes I make this cake even more eye-catching by coloring the whipped cream, too. Use whatever sherbet flavor combination you like.
—Bonnie Hawkins, Elkhorn, WI

Prep: 25 min. + freezing
Makes: 12 servings

- 1 prepared angel food cake (8 to 10 oz.)
- 3 cups rainbow sherbet, softened if necessary

WHIPPED CREAM
- 2 cups heavy whipping cream
- ⅓ cup confectioners' sugar
- 1 tsp. vanilla extract

1. Using a long serrated knife, cut cake horizontally into 4 layers. Place bottom layer on a freezer-safe serving plate; spread with 1 cup sherbet. Repeat twice with middle cake layers and remaining sherbet. Top with remaining cake layer. Freeze, covered, until sherbet is firm, about 1 hour.
2. In a large bowl, beat the cream until it begins to thicken. Add the confectioners' sugar and vanilla; beat until soft peaks form. Frost top and sides of cake. Freeze until firm.
3. Thaw in refrigerator 30 minutes before serving. Cut cake with a serrated knife.
1 piece: 253 cal., 16g fat (10g sat. fat), 54mg chol., 174mg sod., 27g carb. (12g sugars, 2g fiber), 2g pro.

READER REVIEW
"This is a beautiful, unique looking, tasty dessert. It was a hit, and everyone oohed and aahed at it. I love this recipe, and it will be made many times."
—ILUVBOBCATS TASTEOFHOME.COM

CINNAMON MONKEY BREAD

CINNAMON MONKEY BREAD

Is it possible for four kids to cook together without total chaos in the kitchen? Yes, with the right recipe. This is a favorite with my bunch. They get to play with the dough as they roll pieces of refrigerated biscuits into balls. Then, they get to enjoy the results!
—Lisa Combs, Greenville, OH

Prep: 20 min. • **Bake:** 35 min.
Makes: 16 servings

- 4 tubes (7½ oz. each) refrigerated buttermilk biscuits
- ½ cup sugar
- 2 tsp. ground cinnamon
- ½ cup butter, melted
- ½ cup packed brown sugar

1. Preheat oven to 350° Cut each biscuit into 4 pieces; shape into balls. In a small bowl, combine sugar and cinnamon. Roll each ball in the cinnamon sugar. Arrange evenly in a generously greased 9- or 10-in. fluted tube pan. Sprinkle with remaining cinnamon sugar.
2. Combine butter and brown sugar; pour over the top. Place the tube pan on baking sheet; bake until dough is golden brown and cooked through, 35-45 minutes. Cool for 5 minutes before inverting bread onto a serving platter.
1 piece: 133 cal., 6g fat (4g sat. fat), 15mg chol., 174mg sod., 19g carb. (13g sugars, 0 fiber), 1g pro.

❄ RED VELVET CAKE BITES

Everyone loves red velvet, but any cake mix can work. Whatever you do, have fun!
—Anne Powers, Munford, AL

- -

Prep: 45 min. + chilling
Bake: 25 min. + cooling
Makes: 5 dozen

- 1   pkg. red velvet cake
      mix (regular size)
- 1   can (16 oz.) cream cheese frosting
- 1   lb. each white, milk chocolate and
      dark chocolate candy coating

1. Prepare and bake cake mix according to the package directions, using a 13x9-in. baking pan. Cool completely.
2. Crumble cake into a large bowl. Add frosting; beat well. Refrigerate until easy to handle, about 1 hour. Shape into 1½-in. balls; transfer balls to waxed paper-lined baking sheets. Refrigerate at least 1 hour.
3. In a microwave, melt white candy coating; stir until smooth. Dip 20 cake balls into coating; allow excess to drip off. Return to baking sheets; let stand until set. Repeat with milk chocolate and dark chocolate coatings and the remaining cake balls. If desired, drizzle with additional candy coating. Store in airtight containers.

Freeze option: Freeze uncoated cake balls in freezer containers, layered between waxed paper. To use, thaw in covered containers. Dip into coatings as directed.
Note: Candy coating is also known as confectionary coating. This candymaking product is tempered, ready for melting and sets up quickly at room temperature. It's available for purchase in blocks or discs at grocery stores in white, milk and dark chocolate and butterscotch flavors.
1 cake ball: 206 cal., 11g fat (7g sat. fat), 11mg chol., 79mg sod., 28g carb. (24g sugars, 0 fiber), 1g pro.

TEST KITCHEN TIP

To make it easier to more evenly dip the cake balls into the chocolate candy coatings, try using using tooth picks or a wooden skewer.

SLOW-COOKER STRAWBERRY PUDDING CAKE

This recipe was created due to my love of strawberry cheesecake. I had these ingredients in my pantry and thought I'd give it a whirl. The flavors are just like strawberry cheesecake, only in a warm, comforting cake version.
—Lisa Renshaw, KS City, MO

- -

Prep: 20 min. • **Cook:** 4 hours + standing
Makes: 10 servings

- 3   cups cold 2% milk
- 1   pkg. (3.4 oz.) instant cheesecake
       or vanilla pudding mix
- 1   pkg. strawberry cake
       mix (regular size)
- 1   cup water
- 3   large eggs, room temperature
- ⅓   cup canola oil
- 2   cups toasted coconut
       marshmallows, quartered
       Optional: Strawberry ice cream
       topping and sliced fresh
       strawberries

1. In a large bowl, whisk the milk and pudding mix for 2 minutes. Transfer to a greased 4- or 5-qt. slow cooker. Prepare cake mix batter according to package directions with the water, eggs and oil; pour over pudding layer.
2. Cook, covered, on low until edges of cake are golden brown (center will be moist), about 4 hours.
3. Remove slow-cooker insert; sprinkle cake with marshmallows. Let the cake stand, uncovered, for 10 minutes before serving. If desired, serve with ice cream topping and strawberries.
1 serving: 377 cal., 13g fat (4g sat. fat), 62mg chol., 540mg sod., 56g carb. (37g sugars, 1g fiber), 6g pro.

RED VELVET
CAKE BITES

SOPAIPILLAS

SOPAIPILLAS

Light, crispy pastry puffs, sopaipillas are a sweet way to round out a spicy meal. We love to serve them warm and top them off with honey or sugar.
—Mary Anne McWhirter, Pearland, TX

Prep: 15 min. + standing • **Cook:** 25 min.
Makes: 1 dozen

- 1   cup all-purpose flour
- 1½ tsp. baking powder
- ¼   tsp. salt
- 1   Tbsp. shortening
- ⅓   cup warm water
-      Oil for deep-fat frying
-      Honey, optional
-      Confectioners' sugar, optional

1. In a large bowl, combine flour, baking powder and salt. Cut in shortening until mixture resembles fine crumbs. Gradually add water, tossing with a fork until a loose ball forms (dough will be crumbly).
2. On a lightly floured surface, knead the dough for 3 minutes or until smooth. Cover and let rest for 10 minutes. Roll out into a 12x10-in. rectangle. Cut into 12 squares with a knife or cut into 12 circles using a round biscuit cutter.
3. In a deep-fat fryer, heat 2 in. oil to 375°. Fry sopaipillas for 1-2 minutes on each side. Drain on paper towels; keep warm. If desired, serve with honey and/or dust with confectioners' sugar.
1 sopaipilla: 57 cal., 2g fat (0 sat. fat), 0 chol., 109mg sod., 8g carb. (0 sugars, 0 fiber), 1g pro.

READER REVIEW
"These were so easy to make, and it was nice to be able to make them at home!"
—MOMOF4KIDS, TASTEOFHOME.COM

APPLE-SPICE
ANGEL FOOD CAKE

APPLE-SPICE ANGEL FOOD CAKE

Angel food cake mix is lower in fat and calories than regular cake mix. Apple pie spice and toasted nuts add a festive fall flavor.
—Joan Buehnerkemper, Teutopolis, IL

Prep: 10 min. • **Bake:** 35 min. + cooling
Makes: 16 servings

- 1   pkg. (16 oz.) angel food cake mix
- 1   cup water
- ⅔   cup unsweetened applesauce
- ½   cup finely chopped pecans, toasted
- 1   tsp. apple pie spice
-      Reduced-fat whipped topping and/or apple slices, optional

1. In a large bowl, combine cake mix and water. Beat on low speed for 30 seconds. Beat on medium speed for 1 minute. Fold in the applesauce, pecans and pie spice.

2. Gently spoon into an ungreased 10-in. tube pan. Cut through batter with a knife to remove air pockets. Bake on the lowest oven rack at 350° 35-45 minutes or until lightly browned and the entire top appears dry. Immediately invert the pan; cool cake completely, about 1 hour.
3. Run a knife around the side and center tube of pan. Remove the cake to a serving plate. Garnish with whipped topping and/or apple slices if desired.
1 piece: 136 cal., 3g fat (0 sat. fat), 0 chol., 209mg sod., 26g carb. (14g sugars, 1g fiber), 3g pro. **Diabetic exchanges:** 1½ starch, ½ fat.

FIVE-MINUTE BLUEBERRY PIE

DOUGHNUT HOLE CAKE

This is the easiest, most impressive cake I have ever made! You can use chocolate, lemon or strawberry cake mix in place of the red velvet.
—Robert Pickart, Chicago, IL

- -

Prep: 15 min. • **Bake:** 35 min. + cooling
Makes: 16 servings

- 32 vanilla cake doughnut holes
- 1 pkg. red velvet cake mix (regular size)
- 1 can (16 oz.) vanilla frosting

1. Preheat oven to 350°. Place 16 doughnut holes in each of the 2 greased 8-in. round baking pans. Prepare cake mix according to package directions. Pour batter over doughnuts, dividing evenly.
2. Bake until a toothpick inserted in cake comes out clean, 35-40 minutes. Cool in pans for 10 minutes before removing to a wire rack to cool completely. Spread frosting between layers and over top of cake.

1 piece: 420 cal., 20g fat (7g sat. fat), 38mg chol., 401mg sod., 57g carb. (36g sugars, 1g fiber), 4g pro.

GOLDEN POUND CAKE

The surprise ingredient in this cake is a can of Mountain Dew. I sometimes substitute orange cake mix and orange soda for a flavorful variation.
—Vicki Boyd, Mechanicsvlle, VA

- -

Prep: 10 min. • **Bake:** 45 min. + cooling
Makes: 12 servings

- 1 pkg. lemon cake mix (regular size)
- 1 pkg. (3.4 oz.) instant vanilla pudding mix
- 4 large eggs, room temperature
- ¾ cup canola oil
- 1 can (12 oz.) Mountain Dew
  Confectioners' sugar, optional

1. Preheat oven to 350°. In a large bowl, combine cake mix, pudding mix, eggs, oil and soda; beat on low speed 30 seconds. Beat on medium 2 minutes.
2. Pour into a greased and floured 10-in. fluted tube pan. Bake 45-50 minutes or until a toothpick inserted in the center comes out clean. Cool 10 minutes before removing from pan to a wire rack to cool completely. Dust with confectioners' sugar if desired.

1 piece: 363 cal., 19g fat (4g sat. fat), 71mg chol., 413mg sod., 46g carb. (29g sugars, 1g fiber), 4g pro.

FIVE-MINUTE BLUEBERRY PIE

If you like the taste of fresh blueberries, you'll love this pie. Since it's a breeze to whip up, I make it often, especially in summer.
—Milda Anderson, Osceola, WI

- -

Prep: 15 min. + chilling
Makes: 8 servings

- ½ cup sugar
- 2 Tbsp. cornstarch
- ¾ cup water
- 4 cups fresh or frozen blueberries, thawed
- 1 graham cracker crust (9 in.)
  Whipped cream, optional

In a large saucepan, combine sugar and cornstarch. Stir in the water until smooth. Bring to a boil over medium heat; cook and stir for 2 minutes. Add blueberries. Cook for 3 minutes, stirring occasionally. Pour filling into crust. Chill. Garnish with whipped cream if desired.

1 piece: 202 cal., 6g fat (1g sat. fat), 0 chol., 122mg sod., 39g carb. (29g sugars, 2g fiber), 1g pro.

DOUGHNUT
HOLE CAKE

STRAWBERRY POKE CAKE

STRAWBERRY POKE CAKE

Strawberry shortcake takes on a wonderful new twist with this super simple recipe. Strawberries liven up each pretty slice.
—Mary Jo Griggs, West Bend, WI

Prep: 25 min. • **Bake:** 25 min. + chilling
Makes: 12 servings

- 1 pkg. white cake mix (regular size)
- 1¼ cups water
- 2 large eggs, room temperature
- ¼ cup canola oil
- 2 pkg. (10 oz. each) frozen sweetened sliced strawberries, thawed
- 2 pkg. (3 oz. each) strawberry gelatin
- 1 carton (12 oz.) frozen whipped topping, thawed, divided
  Fresh strawberries, optional

1. Preheat oven to 350°. In a large bowl, combine the cake mix, water, eggs and oil; beat on low speed for 30 seconds. Beat on medium for 2 minutes.
2. Pour into 2 greased and floured 9-in. round baking pans. Bake 25-35 minutes or until a toothpick inserted in the center comes out clean. Cool cakes 10 minutes; remove from pans to wire racks to cool the cakes completely.
3. Using a serrated knife, level tops of cakes if necessary. Return layers, top side up, to 2 clean 9-in. round baking pans. Pierce cakes with a meat fork or wooden skewer at ½-in. intervals.
4. Drain juice from strawberries into a 2-cup measuring cup; refrigerate the berries. Add water to juice to measure 2 cups and pour into a small saucepan. Bring to a boil; stir in the gelatin until dissolved. Chill for 30 minutes. Gently spoon over each cake layer. Chill for 2-3 hours.
5. Dip the bottom of 1 pan into warm water for 10 seconds. Invert cake onto a serving platter. Top with chilled strawberries and 1 cup whipped topping. Place second cake layer over topping.
6. Frost the cake with remaining whipped topping. Chill for at least 1 hour. If desired, servewith berries. Refrigerate leftovers.
Note: This cake was tested with Pillsbury white cake mix.
1 piece: 376 cal., 14g fat (7g sat. fat), 35mg chol., 301mg sod., 56g carb. (37g sugars, 1g fiber), 4g pro

TOASTED COCONUT MILK SHAKES

TOASTED COCONUT MILKSHAKES

I created this recipe as a reminder of my oldest brother, Brad, who was a picky eater who loved any dessert with coconut. It has a short list of ingredients, but it's certainly tall on coconut flavor!
—Laurie Hudson, Westville, FL

Takes: 15 min. • **Makes:** 4 servings

- ½ cup flaked coconut
- ⅔ cup coconut milk, stirred before measuring then chilled
- ½ cup cream of coconut, stirred before measuring then chilled
- 4 cups vanilla ice cream
  Sweetened whipped cream

1. In a small skillet, cook and stir the coconut over medium-low heat until toasted, 6-8 minutes. Cool completely.
2. Place coconut milk, cream of coconut, ¼ cup toasted coconut and ice cream in a blender; cover and process until blended.
3. Pour into 4 glasses. Top with whipped cream; sprinkle with remaining coconut. Serve immediately.
1 cup: 502 cal., 30g fat (23g sat. fat), 58mg chol., 161mg sod., 54g carb. (51g sugars, 1g fiber), 6g pro.

PEACH CRISP DELIGHT

I love crisps, and this one is a cinch to whip up. The Rice Chex makes it unique, while the peaches and brown sugar provide loads of classic appeal. Better still, it takes less than 30 minutes from start to finish!
—Tracy Golder, Bloomsburg, PA

Takes: 25 min. • **Makes:** 6 servings

- 2 cans (15 oz. each) sliced peaches, drained
- 2 cups Rice Chex, crushed
- ⅓ cup packed brown sugar
- ¼ cup all-purpose flour
- 3 Tbsp. cold butter
  Whipped topping or ice cream, optional

1. Place peaches in a greased 8-in. square baking dish. In a small bowl, combine the cereal, brown sugar and flour; cut in butter until mixture resembles coarse crumbs. Sprinkle over peaches.
2. Bake the crisp, uncovered, at 375° for 15-20 minutes or until topping is golden brown. Serve warm.
1 serving: 222 cal., 6g fat (4g sat. fat), 15mg chol., 125mg sod., 41g carb. (30g sugars, 1g fiber), 1g pro.

⏱ MILKY WAY PUDGY PIE

My favorite pudgy pies have Milky Way candy bars, graham cracker crumbs and marshmallows. So irresistible. And buttered bread is a must.
—Susan Hein, Burlington, WI

Takes: 10 min. • **Makes:** 1 serving

- 1 Tbsp. butter, softened
- 2 slices white bread
- 1 Tbsp. graham cracker crumbs
- 1 fun-size Milky Way candy bar, chopped
- 2 Tbsp. miniature marshmallows

1. Spread butter over bread slices. Place 1 slice in a sandwich iron, buttered side down. Top with cracker crumbs, chopped candy, marshmallows and the remaining bread slice, buttered side up. Close iron.
2. Cook over a hot campfire until golden brown and marshmallows are melted, 3-6 minutes, turning occasionally.
1 sandwich: 380 cal., 17g fat (10g sat. fat), 32mg chol., 438mg sod., 51g carb. (19g sugars, 2g fiber), 6g pro.

FLOURLESS
CHOCOLATE TORTE

FLOURLESS CHOCOLATE TORTE

Here's the perfect dessert for chocoholics like me. I bake the melt-in-your-mouth torte all the time. For an elegant finish, dust it with confectioners' sugar.
—Kayla Albrecht, Freeport, IL

Prep: 20 min. • **Bake:** 40 min. + cooling
Makes: 12 servings

- 5 large eggs, separated
- 12 oz. semisweet chocolate, chopped
- ¾ cup butter, cubed
- ¼ tsp. cream of tartar
- ½ cup sugar
  Confectioners' sugar, optional

1. Place egg whites in a large bowl; let eggs whites stand at room temperature for 30 minutes. Preheat oven to 350°. In top of a double boiler or a metal bowl over barely simmering water, melt chocolate and butter; stir until smooth. Remove from heat; cool slightly.
2. In another large bowl, beat egg yolks until thick and lemon-colored. Beat in chocolate mixture. With clean beaters, beat egg whites and cream of tartar on medium speed until foamy.
3. Gradually add sugar, 1 Tbsp. at a time, beating on high after each addition until sugar is dissolved. Continue beating until stiff glossy peaks form. Fold a fourth of egg whites into chocolate mixture, then fold in remaining whites.
4. Transfer to a greased 9-in. springform pan. Bake until a toothpick inserted in center comes out with moist crumbs, 40-45 minutes (do not overbake). Cool completely on a wire rack.
5. Loosen sides from pan with a knife. Remove rim from pan. If desired, dust with confectioners' sugar.
1 piece: 326 cal., 24g fat (14g sat. fat), 108mg chol., 121mg sod., 15g carb. (14g sugars, 1g fiber), 5g pro.

RECIPE INDEX

A

Air-Fryer Chicken Thighs, 74
Ambrosia Salad, 38
Appetizer Shrimp Kabobs, 24
Apple-Gouda Pigs in a Blanket, 30
Apple Pie a la Mode, 99
Apple-Spice Angel Food Cake, 105
Artichoke Chicken Pesto Pizza, 76
Asian Ramen Shrimp Soup, 55

B

Bacon & Egg Gravy, 12
Bacon Breakfast Casserole, 17
Baked Asparagus Dip, 28
Baked Ham with Pineapple, 74
Baked Swiss Chicken, 66
Banana Chip Pancakes, 8
Bean Burritos, 69
Beef & Rice Enchiladas, 63
Beef Steaks with Blue Cheese, 63
Berry Dream Cake, 99
Best-Ever Lamb Chops, 79
Big Kahuna Pizza, 64
Birthday Cake Fudge, 93
Blood Orange Caramel
   Tarte Tatin, 100
Breakfast Wraps, 18
Broccoli with Garlic, Bacon
   & Parmesan, 37
Buffalo Chicken Sliders, 54
Buttery Carrots, 35

C

California Dream Smoothie, 19
Candied Walnuts, 22
Caprese Chicken with Bacon, 77
Cheddar-Ham Oven Omelet, 14
Cheeseburger Omelet Sliders, 15
Cheesy Bacon Spaghetti Squash, 38
Cheesy Black Bean Nachos, 71
Cheesy Caramelized Onion
   Skillet Bread, 28
Cheesy Hash Brown Bake, 10
Cheesy Wild Rice Soup, 50
Cherry Cream Cheese Tarts, 100
Cherry Crumb Dessert Bars, 83
Cherry Syrup, 15
Chili & Jelly Meatballs, 30
Chipotle Pomegranate Pulled Pork, 57
Chocolate-Caramel Truffles, 93
Chocolate Molten Cakes, 100

Chocolaty S'mores Bars, 91
Cinnamon Monkey Bread, 101
Cinnamon Tea Rolls, 15
Citrus Avocado Spinach Salad, 45
Classic Avocado Toast, 12
Coconut Pecan Rolls, 17
Comforting Carrot Casserole, 43
Contest-Winning Barbecued
   Pork Chops, 71
Contest-Winning Zucchini
   Pancakes, 44
Cream Cheese Mashed Potatoes, 44
Creamed Corn, 41
Creamy Baked Eggs, 17
Creamy Jalapeno Corn, 35
Creamy Skillet Noodles with Peas, 36
Creamy Wasabi Spread, 28
Cuban Breakfast Sandwiches, 8

D

Doughnut Hole Cake, 106

E

Easy Butternut Squash Soup, 52
Easy Chicken Pesto Stuffed
   Peppers, 68
Easy Chicken Strips, 64
Easy Key Lime Pie, 100

F

Fast Baked Fish, 73
Five-Minute Blueberry Pie, 106
Flourless Chocolate Torte, 110
Fresh Corn Omelet, 10

G

Garlic Bread Pizza Sandwiches, 54
Garlic-Herb Mini Quiches, 27
Garlic Loaf, 41
German Potato Omelet, 19
Ginger-Glazed Grilled Salmon, 65
Ginger-Orange Refresher, 25
Golden Pound Cake, 106
Gourmet Barbecue Beef
   Sandwiches, 52
Grandma's Pressure-Cooker
   Chicken Noodle Soup, 57
Grandma's Tomato Soup, 49
Grandmother's Orange Salad, 43
Green Chile Posole, 51
Grilled Pineapple Chicken, 73

Grits & Bacon Casserole, 11
Gumbo in a Jiffy, 58

H

Ham & Cheese Pockets, 58
Hawaiian Sausage Subs, 55
Homemade Fry Bread, 45
Homemade Holiday
   Marshmallows, 83
Honey Horseradish Dip, 27

I

Insalata Caprese, 40
Italian Grilled Cheese Sandwiches, 50

K

Kalua Pork, 73

L

Lemon-Garlic Salmon Steaks, 72
Lemon Snowflakes, 84

M

Magic Brownie Bars, 91
Maple-Bacon White Chocolate
   Fudge, 86
Maple Pork Ribs, 64
Marinara-Mozzarella Dip, 30
Milk-and-Honey White Bread, 37
Milky Way Pudgy Pie, 110
Minty Peas & Onions, 43
Muffin-Tin Lasagnas, 72

N

No-Bake Cereal Bars, 90

O

Orange Crispies, 84
Orange-Glazed Bacon, 8
Oven-Roasted Potatoes, 41
Overnight Peach Oatmeal, 14

P

Parmesan Pork Medallions, 77
Peach Crisp Delight, 109
Peanut Butter Candy, 84
Peanut Butter Chocolate Bars, 86
Peanut Butter Clusters, 90
Peanut Butter Cookie Cups, 95
Pear & Blue Cheese Salad, 36
Pesto Hamburgers, 50

Pigs in a Blanket, 54
Pina Colada Carrot Salad, 38
Plantain Fritters, 40
Polenta Chili Casserole, 76
Polka-Dot Macaroons, 95
Potato Chip Bites, 89
Pressure-Cooker Buffalo Wing
    Potatoes, 36
Prosciutto-Wrapped Asparagus with
    Raspberry Sauce, 25
Pulled Pork Sandwiches, 49

R
Rainbow Sherbet Angel
    Food Cake, 101
Ranch Potato Salad, 43
Raspberry Almond Strips, 95
Raspberry Chicken, 76
Red Velvet Cake Bites, 102
Roast Beef & Gravy, 74
Roasted Buffalo Cauliflower Bites, 25

S
Saucy Baked Chicken, 68
Sausage & Pepper Sheet-Pan
    Sandwiches, 59
Sausage & Sauerkraut, 74
Sausage & Spinach Calzones, 59
Sausage Bacon Bites, 14

Savory Cucumber Sandwiches, 27
Scallops in Sage Cream, 66
Shrimp Pasta Alfredo, 79
Simmered Smoked Links, 27
Simple Biscuits, 35
Skillet Mac & Cheese, 44
Slow-Cooked Potatoes with
    Spring Onions, 38
Slow-Cooker Cheese Dip, 29
Slow-Cooker Strawberry
    Pudding Cake, 102
Sopaipillas, 105
South Dakota Frito Treats, 84
Sparkling Coconut Grape Juice, 29
Sparkling Peach Bellinis, 8
Special Pork Chops, 65
Special Stuffed Strawberries, 24
Spicy Chicken Nuggets, 79
Spinach & Turkey Pinwheels, 22
Spring Pea Soup, 49
Sticky Honey Chicken Wings, 22
Strawberry Feta Tossed Salad, 41
Strawberry Poke Cake, 109
Sweet & Spicy Peanut Butter-Bacon
    Sandwiches, 49
Sweet & Spicy Pineapple Chicken
    Sandwiches, 51

T
Tangy Beef Turnovers, 79
Tiger Butter Fudge, 95
Toasted Coconut Milk Shakes, 109
Toffee Turtle Squares, 89
Tomato-Basil Pita Pizzas, 63
Tomato Sandwiches, 51
Tortellini with Sausage &
    Mascarpone, 69
Tropical Berry Smoothies, 12
Turkey Breakfast Sausage, 18
Turkey Tenderloin & Root Veggie
    Sheet-Pan Supper, 66

U
Upside-Down Bacon Pancake, 11

V
Vanilla Meringue Cookies, 90

W
White Bean & Chicken Chili, 57

Z
Zippy Praline Bacon, 12